THE OTHER SON OF MAN
Ezekiel/Jesus

THE OTHER SON OF MAN
Ezekiel/Jesus

by
Andrew W. Blackwood, Jr.

BAKER BOOK HOUSE
Grand Rapids, Michigan

Library of Congress Catalog Card Number: 66-27967

PRINTED IN THE UNITED STATES OF AMERICA

To the Congregation

Acknowledgments

The following authors and publishers have graciously given permission to quote from copyright material:

Alfred A. Knopf, New York.
A Bell for Adano, John Hersey. 1944.

Basil Blackwell, Oxford.
He That Cometh, Sigmund Mowinckel. 1956. Translated by G. W. Anderson.

Federal Bureau of Investigation,
Annual Crime Report, Uniform Crime Reports Bulletin, 1963.

The Macmillan Company, New York.
On Her Majesty's Secret Service, Ian Fleming.

The Macmillan Company, New York.
A Theological Word Book of the Bible, Edited by Alan Richardson, *"Son of Man"* by J. Y. Campbell.

Ian Cowie,
Manse Mail, Edinburgh, Issue of May, 1965.
How to Become a Hypocrite.

Methuen & Co., Ltd., London.
The Ezra Apocalypse, W. O. E. Esterly.

Oxford University Press, Inc., New York.
The Scrolls from the Dead Sea, Edmund Wilson.

Bertrand Russell,
The Sunday Times, London,
The Saturday Review, New York, Issue of December 21, 1957.
Can Scientific Man Survive?

8

Charles Scribner's Sons, New York.
In the Secret Place of the Most High, Arthur John Gossip.
1947.

Westminster Press, Philadelphia.
The Son of Man in the Synoptic Tradition, Heinz Tödt.
Tr. D. M. Barton, Copyright SCM Press Ltd., 1965,
Published U.S.A. 1965.

Yale University Press, New Haven.
Faces in the Crowd, David Riesman.

Contents

Foreword

Even a tepid admirer of Ezekiel discovers rapidly that many consider his enthusiasm strange and unaccountable; for, to put it charitably, Ezekiel does not appeal to contemporary taste. Valuable books about the great prophets do not accord to Ezekiel so much as a footnote. I admit readily that others outrank Ezekiel in important respects, yet I call your attention to a curiously neglected fact: Jesus, who certainly was influenced by the other prophets, chose to associate His work with Ezekiel's by a strange self-designation, "Son of Man," a term that appears rarely in the rest of the Old Testament, but eighty-seven times in Ezekiel.

The extent to which the modern world neglects Ezekiel as the Son of Man may be gauged from a profound, scholarly work, recently translated into English, by Heinz Eduard Tödt, *The Son of Man in the Synoptic Tradition*. The massive index of biblical and extra-canonical references runs to six pages in small type. In all this voluminous index is one reference to Ezekiel, which I solemnly quote:

> In Rev. 19.11 the motif of the opened heaven is clearly part of the form of the vision, as is evident from the basic passage Ezekiel 1.1. (Page 304.)

That is, a writer who is seeking to understand what "Son of Man" meant a generation after Jesus' time pays practically no attention to the biblical source from which, I believe, Jesus drew the expression. Dr. Tödt's interest lies in the post-Easter meaning of a term, mine in the pre-Easter meaning. It is not surprising that we who ask different questions receive different answers. But it is surprising that an eminent scholar should ignore evidence that is open to public examination. The fact that Ezekiel belonged to the canonical Scripture in Jesus' day would seem to require one who writes

11

about the subject to demonstrate conclusively that Jesus and the evangelists were *not* alluding to Ezekiel as the earlier Son of Man, if he believes this to be the case.

The belief that Jesus derived His self-designation from Ezekiel is not exclusively mine. (It is remarkably difficult to be original in writing about something that has been under discussion for twenty centuries.) For example, Dr. J. Y. Campbell, Professor of New Testament at Westminster College, Cambridge, discusses the fact, strange to us, that Jesus did not define the term, and that apparently nobody asked Him to explain it. Dr. Campbell says:

> This difficulty is best met if Jesus' use of the phrase is understood in the light of the frequent use of it in Ezekiel, where the prophet is addressed by God as 'Son of Man.' There, too, the meaning of the term is not explained, but no explanation seems to be needed—it suggests at once the littleness of the prophet as a man, and the greatness to which God calls him in his service; through him, man though he is, God speaks to men, and carries out His high purpose.
>
> "Son of Man," **A Theological Word Book of the Bible.**
> Pages 231-232.

In *Hastings' Dictionary of the Bible* we find an interesting comment about "Son of Man."

> There lay in the use of the title by Jesus, at once the idea of the reality and truth of His humanity, the consciousness of His unique perfection as man, the sense of His universal relation to the race, and the knowledge of His calling and function to be the Messianic King. He was the Son of Man, as embodying in Himself the divine idea of a godlike humanity—the Son of Man as the unique individual of the race who sustained this character—the Son of Man in the universal sense, as representing in His Person not the seed of Abraham alone, but the whole of mankind. This title, accordingly, already expresses the principle of the universality of the new religion in its contrast with the national limitations of Judaism.
>
> Volume ii, page 850.

This profound interpretation reflects nineteen centuries of Christian thought, as influenced by Greek philosophy. All these ideas are implicit in the title. This is what "Son of Man" means to Dr. Hastings, to me, and I hope to you, but we may safely say this is not what the term meant to Peter, James, John, and Caiaphas. Without denying any valid philosophic or theological inference that may be drawn, we may turn to literary and historical sources to discover what His contemporaries understood when first they heard Jesus call Himself "Son of Man."

In Ezekiel's day the term "Son of Man" had a relatively clear-cut meaning. The Hebrew is *ben 'adam,* which means literally "child of man" or "son of man." But a literal translation does not always convey the nuance of a phrase. Many scholars believe that the meaning could more accurately be expressed "Man," or, with the article, "The Man." In the Hebrew idiom, "son," frequently designates what we call membership in a class; so "son of man" is "member of the class man," or "mortal." A son of wickedness is a wicked person, a son of righteousness is a righteous person, a son of man is a human being. When the Old Testament was translated into Greek, the seventy learned translators rightly or wrongly gave a literal rendering that carried over into the New Testament, where translation slightly changed the meaning. In the Old Testament the emphasis is upon "Man," in the New it is upon "Son."

The title first occurs in the prophecy immediately after Ezekiel's vision of God's overwhelming power, where the contrast is vivid between the irresistible divine strength and the prophet's mortal weakness. Yet the Almighty says, "Son of Man, stand upon your feet and I will speak with you." The Lord entrusted a heavy task to Ezekiel, who knew that his own strength was not sufficient for it. But he knew likewise that God is present in human life where faith in Him is strong, and the Son of Man tried to be faithful.

Between Ezekiel's time and that of Jesus, six long centuries intervened, during which intense religious thought and activity took place. Not surprisingly, "son of man" experienced some startling alterations in meaning, which make it quite difficult to state, with conviction, exactly what the term conveyed to Jesus' hearers. In the Aramaic tongue, which Jesus usually spoke, the phrase is *bar nas,* which means literally the same as the Hebrew, "a child of man," or "a man." The critic Wellhausen maintained (in *Einleitung in die drei ersten Evangelien,* p. 123) that Jesus did not use the term, because it meant simply any man. But the scanty evidence indicates that the phrase was used with emphasis. "The Man" means something quite different from "the man." Jesus intended to convey something about His person or task when He called Himself "The Son of Man," or "The Man."

THE SON OF MAN—TRIUMPHANT

In Psalms 8:4 and 144:3, "son of man" means simply any human being, whose special dignity is that God cares for him. In Psalm 80:17, "the son of man, whom thou madest strong for thyself," refers to Israel, the collective term for God's chosen people. We do not know, of course, exactly when these Psalms were written, but the date is irrelevant to our discussion, because the meaning, whether it refers to an individual or to the community, is compatible with Ezekiel's usage. However, in another place we find a startlingly different connotation:

> Behold, with the clouds of heaven
> there came one like a son of man,
> and he came to the Ancient of Days
> and was presented before him.
> And to him was given dominion
> and glory and kingdom,
> that all peoples, nations, and languages
> should serve him;
> his dominion is an everlasting dominion,
> which shall not pass away,
> and his kingdom one
> that shall not be destroyed.
> Daniel 7:13-14.

Notice the difference: In the Psalms, as in Ezekiel, the Son of Man is struggling, in the present tense. In Daniel the Son of Man is gloriously triumphant, at some point in the future. Jesus used the term to develop this polarity, which Christians express with the symbolic cross and crown.

As scholars have explored the slowly accumulating bulk of material from Jesus' time, they have thus far discovered surprisingly little that bears on our question. The Talmud, which frequently is a gold mine, is completely disappointing in this respect. One passage (Sanhedrin 98a) is of considerable interest to Christians. Rabbi Joshua ben Levi equates the Son of Man with the Messiah, by combining Daniel 7:13 with Zechariah 9:9, and says that if Israel is meritorious, the Messiah (or Son of Man) will come with the clouds of heaven, but if not, He will come lowly, and riding upon an ass. The value of the statement, for our purpose, dwindles considerably when we learn that the good Rabbi worked in the third century A.D.

In the literature we find "Son of Man" used in three apocryphal works: *The Book of Enoch, the Ezra Apocalypse,* and *the Baruch Apocalpyse.* (See *The Apocrypha and Pseudepigrapha of the Old Testament in English,* edited by R. H. Charles, volume II, *Pseudepigrapha.* Oxford, at the Clarendon Press, 1913.) The latter two were demonstrably written after Jerusalem had fallen. Both use the term "Son of Man" in a sense roughly comparable to that in Daniel. This may reflect what W. O. E. Oesterly calls, "Large amounts of floating eschatalogical material which had been handed down by tradition, and which was common popular property." (*The Ezra Apocalypse,* page xli). It is beyond dispute that "large amounts of . . . eschatalogical material" were "floating" through Hebrew society when Jesus began His mission. It is probable that these ideas were loosely linked to the term, "Son of Man." It is open to discussion that Jesus' hearers automatically thought first of eschatalogical concepts when He called Himself by the title Ezekiel had used.

The Book of Enoch may—or possibly may not—be an invaluable aid in determining what "Son of Man" meant to Jesus' hearers. If all the book is pre-Christian, then it provides much information bearing on the question. One section, *The Parables,* contains four terms that are practically interchangeable, all referring to God's coming representative. He is called "The Righteous One" (see Acts 3:14, 7:52, 22:14), "The Elect One" (see Luke 9:35, 23:35), "The Christ," and "The Son of Man." The Son of Man sits upon His throne (62:3), which is God's throne (51:3), from which He exercises universal dominion (62:3, 6), and from which He will deliver the final judgment:

> He sat on the throne of His glory
> And the sum of judgment was given to the Son of Man,
> And He caused the sinners to pass away and He destroyed
>   from off the face of the earth
> All those who had led the world astray.
>
> Enoch 69:27.

Sigmund Mowinckel, in his scholarly study of the Messiah,

He That Cometh, has exhaustively analyzed the pre-Christian usage of the title "Son of Man," relying chiefly upon *The Book of Enoch* for his information. And he has found that:

> Even before the time of the Maccabees . . . ideas about the Son of Man had found their way, together with the new other-worldly eschatology, into certain circles of learned and pious interpreters of the prophets and apocalyptists, and were so widely known that the author of the Similitudes [Parables] in I Enoch (perhaps shortly before 63 B.C.) could assume that the teaching about the Son of Man would be known and accepted among his readers. During that and the following period it was in still wider circulation, and formed part of the eschatological presuppositions in the circles from which Jesus came . . . in Galilee and east of Jordan.
>
> page 418.

According to Dr. Mowinckel the expression implied sixteen over-lapping "Christian" concepts, which is not to say that all sixteen were simultaneously in the mind of everyone who used the term. The reader may refer to *The Book of Enoch,* or to Dr. Mowinckel who meticulously documents his reason for making each statement.

1. He is, in some sense, divine.
2. He is a heavenly being, living with "the Lord of Spirits" (as God is frequently called in Enoch), and with the elect righteous.
3. He is more than a deified man, in that he has always lived on the heavenly plane.
4. Though divine, he is in human form.
5. In some sense he is related to the creative power. He was before the world was made, and he will ultimately be Lord over all that is created.
6. In some way he is connected with paradise.
7. His name implies that he is the ideal pattern for human conduct.
8. He lives now with the elect righteous in heaven.
9. In some sense the righteous dead are identified with him.
10. He is wise and understanding.
11. He will re-establish the original perfection of the

creation. (In the language of theology, he is an eschatalogical figure.)

12. He will be victor in the final struggle against Satan
    and the evil powers.
13. He is now hidden with the Lord of Spirits. When re-
    vealed, he will be seated on his, or God's, throne of
    glory.
14. He will come with the clouds.
15. He is in some way connected with the resurrection.
16. He will be judge of the world.

So impressive is the frequent usage of "Son of Man" in
The Book of Enoch, and so closely is it related to a vital part
of the Christian message, that it used to be the fashion to
ask whether Jesus took the term from Daniel or Enoch.
Dr. Mowinckel correctly rejects the question. Today we have
as common popular property a great deal of floating scientific verbiage. People who discuss "relativity" in modern
society have *derived* the word from Dr. Einstein, but most
acquired it from their environment, not from the scientist,
and many use it in ways that he would not applaud. Jesus
grew in an environment where "Son of Man" was in use.
He adopted the term as His own, and transformed it. Still,
it meant something to His hearers, who came from a comparable environment, before they had embraced the gamut
of His message. It is questionable that most of them understood what Dr. Hastings or Dr. Mowinckel have suggested.
Dr. Tödt warns, "It may be doubted whether a definite set
of concepts concerning the Son of Man was generally accepted in Jewish apocalyptic literature" *(op. cit.* page 30).

The Gospel record is clear that Jesus, on some occasions,
used "Son of Man" in the above-mentioned sense, meaning
the divine Victor, and that, on some occasions, His hearers
clearly understood exactly what He meant. For example:

> "If you are the Christ, tell us." But he said to them, "If I
> tell you, you will not believe . . . . But from now on the Son
> of man shall be seated at the right hand of the power of
> God." And they all said, "Are you the Son of God?"
>
> Luke 22:67-70.

Evidently, "Son of Man" could be understood as a far more
significant term than "Christ" or "Messiah." Indeed, to many

Hebrews at the time, the Messiah was no more than a military hero who would liberate his people from the Romans. But when the elders, chief priests, and scribes understood that Jesus claimed to be "The Son of Man seated at the right hand of the power of God," they equated the term with "Son of God," and declared that Jesus was a blasphemer.

"Son of Man" appears only once outside the Gospels in the New Testament, as Stephen concludes his passionate defense.

> "Which of the prophets did not your fathers persecute? And they killed those who announced beforehand the coming of the Righteous One, whom you have now betrayed and murdered." . . . They ground their teeth against him. But he, full of the Holy Spirit, gazed into heaven and saw the glory of God, and Jesus standing at the right hand of God; and he said, "Behold, I see the heavens opened, and the Son of man standing at the right hand of God."
>
> Acts 7:52-56.

Apparently it was the expression "Son of Man" that triggered the execution. The religious leaders understood what Stephen meant, as they demonstrated by making him the first Christian martyr.

The New Testament record thus shows that Jesus and the early Church used the term "Son of Man" with the sense recorded in Daniel and the apocryphal works mentioned, signifying transcendent power and the ultimate divine victory in which the Son of Man would be the agent. But several considerations lead one to conclude that this truth is not the whole truth.

THE SON OF MAN—SERVANT

The Book of Enoch is, unhappily, a frail staff to lean on. Unquestionably a book of that name was in such widespread use among the Jewish people before the time of Christ that it had a powerful influence upon the New Testament writers. But the book in our hands today is an Ethiopic version, made in the sixth century, evidently translated from the Greek, which in turn was translated from a Hebrew or Aramaic original. The passages about the Son of Man occur so frequently in the Parables (I Enoch 37-71) that one would expect to encounter the phrase in other parts of the book, if the entire work is indeed pre-Christian. Many students, including Dr. Mowinckel, believe that the Parables were composed about 60 B.C. (The strongest argument for a pre-Christian date is the precarious argument from silence: the Parables say nothing about the crucifixion and resurrection.) Other students, of equal competence, believe that the Parables date from the Christian era, and some believe that the "Son of Man" sections are Christian interpolations. (If so, they are more skillfully done than some other interpolations, which glare out even in translation.)

Students practically all agree that the Parables are a composite section, written by more than one author. The Ethiopic version was made by Christians for Christian use. It is possible that the passages in question were influenced by the New Testament, rather than the reverse. Until confirmatory evidence is found, the matter must remain in doubt.

More important, the New Testament shows that the title was not always understood in the transcendent, victorious sense.

> Jesus . . . asked his disciples, "Who do men say that the Son of Man is?" And they said, "Some say John the Baptist, others say Elijah, and others Jeremiah or one of the prophets." He said to them, "But who do you say that I am?" Simon Peter replied, "You are the Christ, the Son of the living God."
>
> Matthew 16:13-16.

Evidently the term did not automatically evoke images of the final divine triumph among Jesus' followers. To Peter "Christ" or "Messiah" was obviously a far more significant expression than "Son of Man," which, in this instance, means "I." In the other case mentioned above, the Hebrew rulers said, in effect: "If you claim to be the Son of Man in the sense that Daniel used the term, then you blaspheme." Unless it was clearly specified that the term had a special significance, it meant something else. (Also, something about Jesus' ministry pointed to "one of the prophets." His message places Him in the glorious prophetic tradition, with Elijah, Isaiah, Jeremiah, Amos, Hosea, and Ezekiel. But the title "Son of Man" points to one, not all, of these giants.)

Further, the evidence of the Dead Sea Scrolls, so called, shows the term in its earth-bound original meaning. I am not aware of its use in the transcendent sense in the manuscripts that have, thus far, been examined. One example, from many, shows that in the immediately pre-Christian world "son of man" still indicated humility.

> Who is able to bear thy glory,
>   and what then is he, the son of man among thy
>   marvelous works;
> what shall one born of woman be accounted before thee?
>   **The Manual of Discipline**, Closing Psalm.

Another example, likewise chosen from many, shows the son of man fully involved in human frailty.

> Man lives in iniquity from the womb,
>   and in faithless guilt to old age,
> I know that righteousness does not belong to a man,
>   nor to a son of man blamelessness of conduct;
> To the Most High God belong all works of righteousness.
>   Thanksgiving Psalm viii.

Most important, Jesus' own use points in diametrically opposite directions. One direction, the transcendent, we have discussed. For example:

> The Son of man will send his angels.   Matthew 13:41.
> The Son of man is to come with his angels in the glory of his Father.   Matthew 16:27.
> In the new world, when the Son of man shall sit on his glorious throne, you who have followed me will also sit on twelve thrones, judging the twelve tribes of Israel.
>   Matthew 19:28.

Consider now the other direction:

> The Son of man has nowhere to lay his head.   Matthew 8:20.
> The Son of man will suffer.   Matthew 17:12.
>
> The Son of man is to be delivered into the hands of men, and they will kill him.   Matthew 17:22.
>
> The Son of man came eating and drinking, and they say, "Behold a glutton and a drunkard, a friend of tax collectors and sinners!"   Matthew 11:19.

The homeless, suffering mortal Son of Man little resembles the Victor to whom the Ancient of Days presents dominion, glory, and kingdom; but worse, he openly bestows friendship on those with whom a religious person cannot have contact.

> Whoever says a word against the Son of man will be forgiven; but whoever speaks against the Holy Spirit will not be forgiven.
>   Matthew 12:32.

It would take us far afield to explore all that the statement implies. But at least it suggests that the Son of Man works on earth as agent for the same Holy Spirit who desires to work in and through other men. The Son of Man insists upon his humility. He is a man among men.

> He who sows the good seed is the Son of man.
>
> Matthew 13:37.

Here the Son of Man is not pictured exercising world-wide dominion; He is a teacher who continues the prophetic tradition by planting ideas among people, where, the parable indicates, His teaching will encounter thorns and briers. (See Ezekiel 2:6.)

> The Son of man came to seek and to save the lost.
>
> Luke 19:10.

Compare this with the task God entrusted to the other Son of Man (Ezekiel 3:16-21), and with the prophet's description of God's concern for His people (Ezekiel 34:11-16). The picture is not that of the triumphant Son of Man coming with the clouds of heaven, but one who toils on the dusty earth, and who expects His followers to toil and, on occasion, to suffer.

> Blessed are you when men hate you, . . . on account of the Son of man! Rejoice in that day, . . . for so their fathers did to the prophets.
>
> Luke 6:22.

No Hebrew, or early Christian, would be reviled for believing in the future, transcendent Son of Man. This belief evidently was widespread throughout Jewish society. But to associate one's self with Jesus—the struggling, suffering Son of Man—that implied rejection, the sort with which a prophet was painfully familiar. (See Ezekiel 20:49 for an example of the contemptuous rejection which can be more painful than physical violence.)

Jesus' "Son of Man" sayings usually point toward the transcendent person whom Daniel pictures, or toward the humble sort of person Ezekiel was. When a biblical term is used in two completely different senses, theologians regard this as a challenge to their ingenuity. So, along with the other "problems" in New Testament study, there is strong, healthy debate today about the sense in which Jesus used the term, the sense in which the evangelists used it, and what it means in the world today. You can profitably study this debate by referring to Dr. Tödt's work, previously mentioned, where the author says wryly, "assumptions have hardened which violently contradict each other" (page 141). Various scholars, using the techniques of higher criticism, have demonstrated to their satisfaction that Jesus did not use the term in one sense or the other, and that the evangelists imposed a strain of thought upon Jesus' teaching. Many of the hardened assumptions are credible, if first you are willing to rewrite the New Testament.

Since, apparently, it is open season for assumption, I will state mine. I believe that the evangelists were human agents chosen by God and guided by the Holy Spirit to deliver the written message that contains practically all of our information about the Savior's earthly life. I believe that God chose men, not computers, each of whom interpreted the Lord's life from a different human perspective, contributing part of himself to the written record, using words and thought-forms that were colored by his personal background. Further, I know that quotation marks are modern invention. And—finally the assumption—I believe that the evangelists tried to report, not distort, what Jesus said. It is simple dishonesty if a teacher uses a term in one sense and his disciple uses it in a completely different sense, attributing that sense to the teacher. I believe that the evangelists were honest men.

We find in the Gospels that Jesus called Himself "Son of Man," sometimes as a substitute for the personal pronoun. Sometimes He used the term in the general sense that Ezekiel used it, to indicate humility. Sometimes he used it in the transcendent sense that Daniel mentions. No teacher of ordinary competence would use an expression with two different meanings if there were not some unifying factor other than the expression itself. Christian faith affirms that Jesus, the humble, suffering, mortal Son of Man is the Christ, the victorious, transcendent, divine Son of Man. We have here no "problem" that is not inherent within the central Christian affirmation, that "the Word became flesh and dwelt among us." How could the divine Victor be the suffering human servant? I do not know, nor does any one else. But a few "Son of Man" sayings illuminate the mystery, by combining in one sentence the transcendent and the earthly meanings.

> The Son of man goes as it is written of him.
>
> Mark 14:21.

Here the person whose death is predicted is described as the One who was promised in the Law and the prophets.

> . . . that you may know that the Son of man has authority on earth to forgive sins. . . .
>
> Mark 2:10.

If you would wrestle with the "problem," then decide in which sense, the divine or the human, Jesus used the term on this occasion.

> The Son of man is Lord even of the Sabbath.
>
> Mark 2:27.

Could a claim be more bold? The Jewish people, on occasion, made a graven image of the Sabbath Day (which in no way justifies our under-valuing its importance). Jesus warned that the aim of human life is not to keep the Sabbath, but the day was ordered because man needs it. And then He made His claim that the Son of Man is Lord of the day. Again, I ask, in which of the two senses was He using the expression?

> When you have lifted up the Son of man, then you will know that I am he, and that I do nothing on my own authority but speak thus as the Father taught me.
>
> John 8:28.

The sentence is meaningless, except as a play on completely different meanings of a term. "When you have crucified the Son of Man [me, Jesus the Carpenter] then you will know that I [Jesus the Carpenter] am he [The Son of Man, triumphant, divine, the Judge of the living and the dead] and I [Jesus the Carpenter] do nothing on my own authority but speak as the Father taught me." The earthling Son of Man thus accepts the prophetic office, with a self-designation that points to Ezekiel more than to any other prophet. (See Ezekiel 13 for an analysis, by negation, of the prophet's task.)

Affirming both aspects of the mystery simultaneously, we find:

As the lightning flashes and lights up the sky from one side to the other, so will the Son of man be in his day. But first he must suffer many things and be rejected by this generation.

Luke 17:24-25.

A key verse in New Testament interpretation shows more clearly than any other what is the link between the homeless, suffering, rejected Son of Man and the triumphant, divine Son of Man who can be pictured in lightning flashes. This verse is found in Mark, which, most critics believe, contains less interpretation by the evangelist than any of the other three Gospels.

The Son of man also came not to be served but to serve, and to give his life as a ransom for many.

Mark 10:45.

Christ's triumph is accomplished, not with pomp and circumstance, but with humility, service, suffering, and death. This strain of thought is usually related to the "Suffering Servant" concept, which is developed with incomparable beauty and profundity in Isaiah 53, for example. But that is not the only place where the idea is developed.

One major book in the Bible is about a suffering servant, despised and rejected of men, a man of sorrows and acquainted with grief, whom God called "Son of Man." He saw brilliant flashes of the divine glory, but he lived and worked amid rejection, crying into deaf ears, working with hands (spiritually) tied, sitting upon (spiritual) scorpions. Yet he kept on doing the will of God, in the place where he was, without external rewards, year after discouraging year. He foresaw a victory—the exiles would return to Jerusalem—and many thought him insane. There was no Jerusalem to return to. Nebuzaradan had destroyed it. Only a madman could dream about return. But Ezekiel held the peculiar madness of faith. He dreamed his dreams. He said his prayers. He worked unremittingly without hope of personal gain, and with no visible results. And his prayer was answered. The exiles returned.

The passage quoted above from *The Book of Enoch* bears a striking resemblance to a far more familiar passage:

> When the Son of man comes in his glory, and all the angels with him, then he will sit on his glorious throne. Before him will be gathered all the nations, and he will separate them one from another as a shepherd separates the sheep from the goats.
>
> Matthew 25:31-32.

As I have indicated, it is debatable whether the form of this passage was influenced by that in Enoch, or the reverse. But another literary source is undebatable. Read Ezekiel 34, from which Jesus almost unquestionably drew His imagery, and, as was His custom, He made more glorious that which already was glorious.

The *Book of Ezekiel* was a part of Holy Scripture in Jesus' time. The content was more familiar to His Jewish auditors than it is to the majority of Christians today. When Jesus called Himself "Son of Man," He could, by defining the term, point to the transcendent concept expressed in Daniel and other places. But it is far more likely that a Jew, hearing the term without explanation, would think first of another to whom God said, "Son of Man, stand upon your feet, and I will speak with you." This fact alone is sufficient reason for seeking to understand the other Son of Man. Jesus looked to Ezekiel as the architect who rebuilt a nation in ruins, and the Carpenter, with Ezekiel's guidance, set out to rebuild a shattered world.

Ezekiel 1:1-28

In the thirtieth year, in the fourth month, on the fifth day of the month, as I was among the exiles by the river Chebar, the heavens were opened, and I saw visions of God.... As I looked, behold, a stormy wind came out of the north, and a great cloud, with brightness round about it, and fire flashing forth continually, and in the midst of the fire, as it were gleaming bronze. And from the midst of it came the likeness of four living creatures. And this was their appearance: they had the form of men, but each had four faces, and each of them had four wings.... Under their wings on their four sides they had human hands.... Their wings touched one another; they went every one straight forward, without turning as they went. As for the likeness of their faces, each had the face of a man in front; the four had the face of a lion on the right side, the four had the face of an ox on the left side, and the four had the face of an eagle at the back.... And each went straight forward; wherever the spirit would go, they went, without turning as they went. In the midst of the living creatures there was something that looked like burning coals of fire, like torches moving to and fro among the living creatures; and the fire was bright, and out of the fire went forth lightning....

Now as I looked at the living creatures, I saw a wheel upon the earth beside the living creatures, one for each of the four of them ... their construction being as it were a wheel within a wheel. When they went, they went in any of their four directions without turning as they went. The four wheels had rims and they had spokes; and their rims were full of eyes round about. And when the living creatures went, the wheels went beside them; and when the living creatures rose from the earth, the wheels rose....

... And when they went, I heard the sound of their wings like the sound of many waters, like the thunder of the Almighty, a sound of tumult like the sound of a host; when they stood still, they let down their wings....

Above the firmament over their heads there was the likeness of a throne, in appearance like sapphire; and seated above the likeness of a throne was a likeness as it were of a human form. And upward from what had the appearance of his loins I saw as it were gleaming bronze, like the appearance of fire enclosed round about; and downward from what had the appearance of his loins I saw as it were the appearance of fire, and there was brightness round about him. Like the appearance of the bow that is in the cloud on the day of rain, so was the appearance of the brightness round about....

And when I saw it, I fell upon my face, and I heard the voice of one speaking.

GLORY SHINES THROUGH
Ezekiel 1:1-28

A young man named Ezekiel, standing by the River Chebar, saw a vision of the living God. It was late in what we would call the month of June, in the year 593 before Christ. A dust storm had swirled out of the desert into the flat, monotonous, irrigated plain where, we may believe, Ezekiel was tilling the small truck garden in which he earned his daily bread. When a dust storm comes most people hide their faces, lest the gritty particles get in their eyes. Ezekiel was an unusual man. He faced the storm, and while its fury buffeted him he saw light and motion and *glory,* as God revealed Himself within the storm cloud.

THE RIVER CHEBAR

An atlas of the ancient world will show you the River Chebar, a large canal to the west of Babylon, in the Tigris-Euphrates irrigation complex. If you will look at any major canal in fertile southern Florida, you can see something resembling that which Ezekiel saw: a wide body of water extending to the horizon on the left and the right. Running to the water's edge is intensive cultivation, acre after flat acre covered with rich green crops. As you look at the canal you may think about the productivity it has brought to land that otherwise would be barren. You may marvel at the engineering that built it. Or you may wonder if it contains any fish. But the canal as such neither draws you close to God nor repels you from Him.

It was not so with young Ezekiel. To him the River Chebar was a vivid symbol for all the bitterness, frustration, and resentment that can fill a man's heart. To him the River Chebar, flowing through the fertile plains of Babylonia, was silently claiming that God had failed. For Ezekiel was an exile, shut away from the land he loved, forbidden to visit the Temple he had known in his boyhood, condemned by an alien king to dwell beside the Chebar.

Why was Ezekiel an exile? The story is written in the second Book of Kings. Nebuchadnezzar, the emperor of Babylon, controlled the little kingdom, Judah. King Jehoiakim rebelled against him. Nebuchadnezzar sent an army against Jerusalem. Jehoiakim died, and his son Jehoiachin came to the perilous throne. He reigned for three miserable months, then surrendered to Nebuchadnezzar, who melted down the golden vessels with which Ezekiel's fathers had worshiped the Lord, and looted other treasures from the royal palace and the Temple. The Babylonian emperor took the leading citizens of Jerusalem, Ezekiel among them, as hostages. He installed a puppet king on the throne, dragged the hostages to Babylon, and turned his mind to other important matters.

To our knowledge, Nebuchadnezzar did not abuse the hostages. Ezekiel's physical surroundings were quite comfortable. The exiles had considerable freedom to move about. They lived in small Hebrew colonies, where they were allowed to practice their various trades. As long as they made no trouble they were unmolested by the police. They had enough to eat. They dressed comfortably. Their houses were respectable. But they were exiles.

The Hebrews had considered Jerusalem the city of God. An alien king had invaded the holy city and pillaged the Temple. Where was God? Was He unable to protect His people? Did He no longer care?

Man must eat to live; so he toils and earns and eats and survives, even when nothing is left to live for. The exiles pounded their brass ware or wove their cloth or hoed their fertile gardens in a sodden, mechanical way and gradually they forgot the past. They had been in Babylon five long years when Ezekiel saw his vision, and many of them were making jokes about the God who had failed. This is what the Chebar meant to Ezekiel. The heart had been wrenched from his life. He was doomed to a biological existence, comfortable enough in its way, until he died and friends laid his body in alien soil. He had grown up believing himself an heir of God's promise to Abraham. The future contained for him no promise, no hope, no God.

In emotional terms of today we might try to describe what the Chebar meant to Ezekiel.

> In the thirty-seventh year of my life, when the third baby was on the way, I opened my pay envelope and drew out a slip saying, "Your services are no longer required."

If this has ever happened to you, you know something about Ezekiel's feelings as he looked at the Chebar.

> On Tuesday afternoon at 2:15 I received a telegram saying, "The Secretary of the Navy regrets to inform you. . . ."

People adjust to the tragedy of death, but a dull ache never quite goes away. Ezekiel was living with this dull ache all the time. The River Chebar reminded him constantly of his loss.

> On January 14, the doctor came to me from my wife's bed-side, and said, "There is nothing more I can do."

Somehow, when a person you love is enduring horrible pro-longed pain, you manage to carry on. Ezekiel was carrying on, doggedly, persistently, while the whole nation he loved was afflicted with a terminal carcinoma.

Or, if you would plumb the utmost depths of despair, you might try being a clergyman today. Two things about a clergyman's work make him want to give up, conscious that his life has been wasted. One is hearing what Christians complain about: people who are called to bear a cross bravely show an incredible ability to bewail trifles. The other is learning what Christians are perfectly willing not to complain about: people who are supposed to follow Christ in compassion for mankind are able blithely to ignore conditions that make the angels weep. Every clergyman I know has, time and again, been in spirit with the Prophet Ezekiel beside the River Chebar.

DESCRIBING THE INDESCRIBABLE

We remember Ezekiel today, not because he shared our common human lot, which includes moments of sheer despair for almost all of us, but because in the darkness he

saw the blazing, dazzling, blinding flame of hope. The lonely
exile by the Chebar saw a dark cloud coming down from
the north. The storm cloud was what people now call a dust-
devil. At some times of day, a dust-devil may be filled with
strange, iridescent colors, as the sun glints against the sand
particles that fill the cloud. Ezekiel watched, afraid but fas-
cinated, while the storm drew closer, and slowly with the
eyes of spiritual vision he began to see shining through the
cloud God's infinite glory.

Ezekiel is nearly blinded by the glory. But most of the
chapter describes the chariot-throne upon which the glory
rides. Kings rode chariots in those days. Ezekiel sees a con-
queror's chariot, coming down from the home of the Babylonian gods who dwelt in the mysterious mountains to the
north.

The first chapter in Ezekiel is almost incomprehensible to
many Christians in the twentieth century. The best they can
do is make bad jokes about the wheels within wheels and
shrug their shoulders. The chapter is written in an alien
tongue, the language of poetic symbolism. If the description of the chariot-throne conveys no more, it should at least
suggest to you that God is mystery inexpressible, before
whom, St. Augustine says, the soul is both ashudder and
aglow.

We cannot describe God. It is sheer blasphemy when people call Him "the Man upstairs" and similar cheap epithets.
The writers of the Holy Bible picture God with poetry and
parable, not the bald language of literal prose. We cannot
pin labels on the infinite. The best we can do is erect signposts, pointing toward Him. The closer we come, the more
we are aware that God is mystery.

Centuries before Ezekiel's vision Moses had a comparable
experience, and he described it thus:

> Moses said, "I pray thee, show me thy glory." And he said, "I
> will make all my goodness pass before you ... but you cannot
> see my face.... Behold, there is a place by me where you shall
> stand ... and while my glory passes by I will put you in a
> cleft of the rock, and I will cover you with my hand until
> I have passed by: then I will take away my hand, and you
> shall see my back; but my face shall not be seen."
>
> Exodus 33:18-23.

Centuries after Ezekiel, the Apostle Paul likewise saw a flash of divine light, and here is his description:

> I know a man in Christ who fourteen years ago was caught up to the third heaven—whether in the body or out of the body I do not know, God knows. And I know that this man was caught up into Paradise—whether in the body or out of the body I do not know, God knows—and he heard things that cannot be told, which man may not utter.
>
> II Corinthians 12:2-4.

Sometimes modern critics sound as if they are saying that such bewildering language is all a mistake that could have been avoided if only the writer had taken more pains to express himself accurately. We are considering some of the greatest writing the world has yet read. We might pay the human authors the compliment of noticing that they can all be painfully intelligible. I doubt if any author has ever written a sentence easier to understand than Moses' curt, "You shall not covet your neighbor's wife." You cannot misunderstand the Apostle Paul when he says, "Love is patient and kind; love is not jealous or boastful; it is not arrogant or rude." And Ezekiel, who can be as baffling as any writer who ever wrote, can say with crystalline lucidity, "Though briers and thorns are with you and you sit upon scorpions, be not afraid."

Why is it that three massive intellects, each writing to persuade us to dedicate our lives to God, can be so understandable on one occasion and so obscure on another? One time they are talking about ethics, the science of right living. Another time they are erecting signposts pointing toward the divine. Christian faith affirms that the divine and the good can be separated only for purposes of discussion, but there is a distinction.

God cannot be reduced to human dimensions and concepts. Always we are trying to whittle God down to a size that we can understand. The prophet Ezekiel presents a workable antidote to this tendency. Again and again he exalts the mystery, but again and again he stresses that God who is exalted far beyond our understanding makes quite unmysterious and thoroughly intelligible claims upon our moral life.

THE LANGUAGE OF SYMBOLISM

The first chapter in Ezekiel is symbolism, designed to help us think magnificently about God. A symbol is the use of one thing to suggest another. We use symbols all the time. They do not greatly trouble us, except when we find them in the Bible. You are driving down the street. A light ahead of you turns from green to red. Why do you stop? It is not written in the stars that red shall mean stop and green go. We have arbitrarily adopted these symbols to help us in the necessary, important business of traffic regulation. On a ship red means starboard and green means port. Why? Centuries ago the sailors of the world agreed on a color code, symbolic aids to navigation. In the United States the colors red and green automatically suggest Christmas. Why? The reasons go back into the pre-Christian religious practices of our Teutonic ancestors in the dark northern forests. With these three facts before us, we can draw a few conclusions about symbols. First, a symbol doesn't need to look or sound or smell or taste or feel like the thing symbolized. All it must do is suggest an idea. Second, a symbol speaks to your imagination. When the helmsman sees a green light in the darkness, he imagines another ship, and can tell in what direction it is going. Third, a symbol can have many meanings, among which you must pick and choose. Do not, for instance, decide that the large red light in the middle of the street is a left-over Christmas ornament.

The other Son of Man used symbolic language all the time. Many of His symbols are so beautiful and so meaningful that our prosaic western minds accept them without a whimper. I am the Door. I am the Bread of Life. I am the Way. I am the Light of the World. I am the true Vine. These word-pictures help us to realize that Christian faith is a personal relationship with Christ, not a set of propositions about Him. We are supposed to be as close to Christ as the branches are to a vine, His thoughts guiding our thoughts, His love filling our hearts. Yet even while we affirm this, we say likewise that Christ is utterly beyond us, far more than the sun is beyond the earth. We take the first faltering steps of Christian life, confident that He will lead us from our mammalian existence to unspeakable eternal glory. He is our link with God, our bridge to eternity. And here I am using symbols. How else can I speak about Christ?

THE SYMBOLS IN EZEKIEL'S VISION

In the rich symbolism of number, four usually represents this world: the four corners of the earth, the four winds, the four seasons. And you will notice that the chariot-throne for the divine glory is described in terms of four. Four living creatures, each with four faces and four wings, pilot the four-wheeled vehicle. Do not abuse the visionary four by treating it as a mathematical expression. Here it means that the glory of God fills the whole earth. He is not confined to the Temple, back in Jerusalem, nor is he enthroned in some distant heaven. He is here, by the River Chebar—or whatever corresponds to the Chebar in your life—conquering and to conquer.

If we try to understand the chariot-throne the way we try to understand the diagram of a gas-turbine engine in *Popular Mechanics,* we shall fail, miserably. If we realize that Ezekiel is helping troubled people to be confident in God, it is enough. The creatures piloting the chariot-throne "each went straight forward; wherever the spirit would go, they went, without turning as they went." How can the chariot-throne go straight in any direction without turning? The kind of chariot that might be described in *Popular Mechanics* couldn't. But God can, and this is a central thought in Ezekiel's prophecy. The words, or the idea, "straight forward," fill the pages that follow.

The lonely prophet must speak about judgment and doom. Bad people have sinned, and good people die horribly. Why? Ezekiel teaches that in the madness of history God is working out His purpose. Unending, unbending, He moves straight forward toward His goal. The other Son of Man reminds us that God cares even for the sparrow that falls. He teaches that no one who loses his biological life while fighting God's battle has actually died. What is really important about him enters the full reality of life after physical existence is over and done with. Ezekiel does not go this far. But he does show that God moves "straight forward" when the eye of flesh can see nothing but the gritty swirling storm-cloud.

The chariot-throne had wheels. A wheel is a meaningful symbol. It moves. In faith we worship not the impassive non-god of the Buddhists, not the Divine Absolute, nor the Class of all Classes, nor the Judeo-Christian tradition, but the God who moves. Yet there was no steering device to turn the wheels. This is another way of saying that the chariot-throne goes "straight forward." God is always new, yet God is always the same. The life of faith, likewise, is always new yet always the same. People act, sometimes, as if Christianity consists of stuffy conventions dreamed up when Victoria was queen. None will deny that stuffy conventions have been confused with spiritual life. But the will of God for human behavior is eternal and unchanging. Circumstances change, but the need remains for faith, integrity, honor, loyalty, and the rest. God does not swerve from His course: neither should we. This is Ezekiel's message to the cynical exiles by the Chebar.

Eyes were on the wheels. The symbol is ludicrous, if you were to attempt a drawing, and glorious if you accept its imaginative value. Eyes are made for seeing. God sees what happens beside the Chebar.

Symbolism is the gateway to the imagination. If Ezekiel's symbolism suggests more to you than it does to me, this means you have a better imagination than mine. I pray you not to be aggrieved with me on that account.

Two symbols are unmistakable: flight and light. Wings, majestic wings, so powerful that their rhythmic pulsations shake the earth, carry the chariot-throne where the Spirit directs. And light, fire, color, radiance and splendor shine on him who is willing to open his spiritual eyes in the midst of the black storm-cloud.

So much for the throne. Seated upon the throne Ezekiel sees:

> A likeness as it were of a human form. And upward from what had the appearance of his loins I saw as it were gleaming bronze . . . and downward from what had the appearance of his loins I saw as it were the appearance of fire, and there was brightness round about him.

The vision is "of God" only in the sense that it comes "from God." Ezekiel does not pretend to see the Maker of heaven and earth. He sees the likeness as the appearance as it were of the divine glory. And yet, this likeness of the appearance of the effulgence surrounding the divine glory has, as it were a human form. God is not a benevolent clergyman with a long grey beard. Our eyes cannot see Him. Our minds cannot picture Him. Our words and our thoughts cannot represent Him. And yet, God more resembles a person than any other reality we can imagine or describe. Personality is the highest moral idea that your mind can encompass. If you can think of a higher idea, let me know, and I will then say that God is more like what you say than like a person. Until then, the Church will continue to follow Ezekiel in thinking that God is one with whom people like us can have personal dealings. We can say, and mean, "Our Father." We could not say this to gravity, morality, or any other force that guides and controls our lives.

Nowadays theologians are saying in language as unintelligible as Ezekiel's that we must quit speaking flippantly and cheaply about God. We must recover the dimension of depth in our religious life. We must not think of God as a Being among other beings, but as the Ground of being. And this is in complete accord with what Ezekiel says, I think more successfully. The Ground of being can say "I." And you, a creature of earth, can say to Him, "Father."

As you read through Ezekiel's difficult, but absorbing, prophecy, you find him referring again and again to the initial vision. His shattering experience of God left on his soul a mark that could not fade. And yet the intellectual content of the vision was familiar to Ezekiel before he saw the storm-cloud. He was a Hebrew. He had the rich heritage of faith as expounded by Moses, David, Amos, Isaiah and many others. He had known all along that God is present both in times when we feel His presence and in times when we do not. He knew perfectly well that God is by the River Chebar. He knew that God is light and life and glory. He knew that God moves straight forward. With his mind Ezekiel knew these things, but faith can never be mere knowledge about God. Faith means knowing God.

Most religious conclusions, when you reduce them to work-a-day prose, sound (God forgive us) tame and unexciting. The other Son of Man said to His disciples, "A new com-

mandment I give to you." Can you imagine the way they
sat up? At last all this complicated business of Christian life
would be made clear to them. "That you love one another."
Can you imagine the way they sagged back, looked at one
another and muttered with disappointment, "Oh, that again."
Perhaps, if we ever catch up with the old, old commandment
to love one another, the Lord will give us another commandment that genuinely is new to our minds.

Ezekiel and his fellow exiles knew the facts of faith. But
when you are off by the River Chebar, your faith sometimes
seems a remote memory from the past. Oh yes, I suppose
it's still true. But I've got to get on with hoeing the onions.
God called Ezekiel, in his daily drudgery, to dedicate his
life, his time, his talents, his everything to God, in a place
and at a time when there appeared no earthly reason to hope
that any good would come of it. God called. Ezekiel answered. And the good came.

God still calls, frequently through the Holy Bible, a prin-
cipal means by which He speaks to man. Embarrassingly
enough, the Bible contains *The Book of Ezekiel,* which, for
seemingly excellent reasons, most of us have studiously ignored. I ask you to read this book, knowing that you will
not understand much of it—at least I don't. I can almost
promise that you will not enjoy the prophecy, for it deals
with the same kind of horror that fills the news today:
treachery, destruction, bloodshed, and stupidity in high places.
You can understand Ezekiel when he is describing these
tragedies, as he does at considerable length and in sanguinary
detail. Keep on reading, through pages that horrify and
disgust you, and gradually the prophets's meaning will become clear. He teaches you to open your eyes while the sand-
storm blows and to see that through the chaos and the
eclipse shines the eternal glory.

Ezekiel 1:28—3:3

When I saw [the appearance of the likeness of the glory of the Lord] I fell upon my face, and I heard the voice of one speaking. And he said to me, "Son of man, stand upon your feet, and I will speak with you." And when he spoke to me the Spirit entered into me and set me upon my feet. . . . And he said to me, "Son of man, I send you to the people of Israel, to a nation of rebels, who have rebelled against me; they and their fathers have transgressed against me to this very day. . . . And you shall say to them, 'Thus says the Lord God.' And whether they hear or refuse to hear (for they are a rebellious house) they will know that there has been a prophet among them. And you, Son of man, be not afraid of them nor . . . of their words, though briers and thorns are with you and you sit upon scorpions; be not afraid of their words, nor be dismayed at their looks, for they are a rebellious house. And you shall speak my words to them, whether they hear or refuse to hear. . . . But you, Son of man . . . be not rebellious like that rebellious house; open your mouth, and eat what I give you." And when I looked, behold, a hand was stretched out to me, and, lo, a written scroll was in it; and he spread it before me; and it had writing on the front and on the back, and there were written on it words of lamentation and mourning and woe. And he said to me, "Son of man, eat what is offered to you; eat this scroll, and go, speak to the house of Israel." . . . Then I ate it; and it was in my mouth as sweet as honey.

THE BURDEN OF FAITH AND
THE STRENGTH TO BEAR IT
Ezekiel 1:28-3:3

Ezekiel had a profound, almost shattering experience by the bank of the Chebar. After the exaltation came the call to duty. Years later, as he was writing his memoirs, the prophet described this call from five different viewpoints, of which we have read two in our Scripture lesson. My own thought is that, after he had seen the vision, Ezekiel returned to his home in Telabib, and stayed there, isolated and silent, while ideas went tumbling pell-mell through his head. The various trips here and there, I believe, took place in thought. They represent different spiritual viewpoints from which Ezekiel looked at his work. In the present arrangement, we find first a clear picture of the burden God laid upon Ezekiel's shoulders, and second a symbolic picture of the strength the Lord gives His disciple so that he can bear the burden.

EZEKIEL'S BURDEN

Ezekiel's task was to deliver a message of judgment to a group of people who believed that already they had been judged over-harshly. Judgment does not necessarily mean condemnation. It means rather God's examination. The right human response to judgment is repentance, which means self-examination, keeping what is good and turning from the evil. The exiles did not want to repent, it is hard work.

The exiles knew the burdens with which our race is familiar: sickness, responsibility, family cares, finances, and the rest. Further, they were exiled for sins they had not committed, while their brothers, who were no better, were

38

living comfortably in Jerusalem. Their masters in exile
were the Babylonians who, after every allowance has been
made for differing customs and traditions, were their moral
inferiors. And to these people Ezekiel was sent with a message: repentance. They wanted the Bible's other message:
consolation.

Running through the Holy Bible is a message of consolation, which I am privileged to express almost every day
that I live. "Underneath are the everlasting arms." "The
Lord is my Shepherd." "Comfort ye, comfort ye, my people."
"Peace I leave with you." "Lo, I am with you alway, even
unto the end of the world." And the most heartening message
ever delivered, "He is risen."

Ezekiel is not renowned for his ministry of consolation, but
even so, he made a wonderful contribution to the Bible,
with his teaching in the thirty-fourth chapter, where the
divine Shepherd says:

> I will seek the lost, and I will bring back the strayed, and
> I will bind up the crippled, and I will strengthen the weak.

The Savior took this passage from Ezekiel and developed it
into one of His most beloved and beautiful parables. Ezekiel's
entire prophecy is consoling, if you read it thoughtfully; for
it proclaims the final victory of God over the Babylonian
captors and every other power that works against Him.

People want, and need, the message of consolation. But
it contains a danger. Like any one-sided emphasis of the
Gospel—or anything else—a truth that is stressed to the ex-
clusion of other truths can become a falsehood. The danger
is that we all want more consolation than we need. Ezekiel's
prophecy, in broad perspective, is consoling, but he tells us,
more than we want to hear, that the final victory will come
only after harsh struggle. Ezekiel is ordained to proclaim
the consoling message, but his more immediate task is to
stir his people to moral responsibility, to self-examination
and repentance where they have been wrong. They are to
be the earthly agents of God's victory, and victory rarely
comes to the sluggish and satisfied.

Frequently in a convalescent home the physician and the
head nurse hold a long, serious discussion. Is this patient
well enough to get up and walk to his meals? Usually they

decide that he should walk long before the patient has reached the decision himself. He complains bitterly that at the rate he is paying he ought to have his meals brought to him. (Actually, this is easier for the staff than requiring the patient to walk to the table.) But they who have more experience know that a person can easily learn to enjoy poor health. For his own recovery he must learn to stand on his feet. This is the message Ezekiel was directed to give to the exiles by the Chebar, and through them to us. It was not a popular message then. It is not popular now.

On the field of battle as the hour for attack draws close, the soldiers crouch in their fox-holes waiting for the sergeant's whistle. A civilian has no idea how comfortable a fox-hole can be with six inches of water in it. The whistle blows. Each soldier can think of a dozen excellent reasons why he ought to remain where he is. So it was in the days of Ezekiel. The exiles could see many reasons why they should feel sorry for themselves. They did not want to face the struggle of repentance. They did not want to bear the burdens of faith or fight the battles of the Lord. They could see with crystalline clarity why the Babylonians ought to repent. For themselves, they wanted Ezekiel to leave them alone.

A young woman was engaged to a strong young man, who was called overseas during the Korean conflict, and who died on Heartbreak Ridge. Is there any who lacks sympathy? She decided to forget her sorrow in a colorful round of riotous living, through which she dragged eight different people into shame, humiliation, and disgrace. When anyone attempted to speak with her, she would snap back, "Don't I have a right to live my own life?" Of course she had a right, not only a right, but an inescapable duty to live her own life.

Once I was writing to someone whom my young friend had bruised and I said, "If only her fiance had lived, today she would be a strong constructive member of society instead of a pathetic wreck." The more I think about my words the emptier they sound. My professor of Logic used to say, "From a hypothesis contrary to fact, any conclusion whatsoever can be validly drawn. If you start from nowhere you will end equally nowhere." The young man did not live. The young woman with a genuine heartbreaking sorrow still was called to live a life acceptable to God. She tried to break His commandments. She succeeded only in breaking herself and hurting eight other people.

So the exiles by the River Chebar wanted nothing of Ezekiel's gloomy warning. They welcomed the message of consolation from the false prophets. They were quite willing to believe in God as long as He was willing to sympathize with them, but they did not want to be told about repentance and righteousness. They had enough trouble already. Only one with a heart of flint could feel no sympathy, yet God's message to them, through the prophet Ezekiel, remains up-to-date. We are called upon to live our faith not under ideal conditions, but under the circumstances where we find ourselves, be it by the River Chebar or in the Valley of the Shadow.

As the Lord commissioned Ezekiel, He warned that the reception would not be cordial:

> And you, Son of man, be not afraid of them, nor be afraid of their words, though briers and thorns are with you and you sit upon scorpions; be not afraid of their words, nor be dismayed at their looks, for they are a rebellious house. And you shall speak my words to them, whether they hear or refuse to hear; for they are a rebellious house.

Ezekiel faced a problem that confronts every clergyman. "Why stir things up? We have enough headaches now without manufacturing any new ones." Almighty God left Ezekiel no choice in the matter. He sent him a directive to stir things up, knowing that the exiles would bitterly resist any change.

Why stir things up? Among the ancient Greek and Roman dramatists, the second-raters used a device called the *deus ex machina*. The plot would get thicker and thicker until no earthly answer was in sight. Then a creaking device would lower an actor representing Zeus or Apollo or some other deity onto the stage, and he would legislate a few miracles. The villain would slink off in disgrace, the hero would marry the beautiful girl, and everyone would be happy. The genuine poets scorned this device. That is not the way God acts. God changes situations, usually, by changing people.

So seriously does God take the necessity for change in us that He went to a Cross to effect it. The Cross is not a magic event long ago that somehow will automatically transport us to heaven when we die. It is the power by which God draws us from our selfishness into His love. Through the Cross He turns our attention from things to people. He helps us to seek not the one who can benefit us but the one who needs our help. He teaches us to desire duty rather than pleasure. Likewise, through the Cross, our Lord teaches us that when we have sinned we must repent. Taking the Cross seriously changes the direction of human life. Before the physical event of the Cross, God sent Ezekiel to change the direction of human lives, because God was planning to change the world.

It is highly pertinent to the religious scene today to ask just what Ezekiel hoped to accomplish and how he hoped to accomplish it. His long-range goal was the political and spiritual independence of the Hebrew people, with complete economic and social justice. Before this could become a reality, he saw with increasing dread that the whole structure of Hebrew society must be smashed. The builders of the new society were a few exiles, living under suspicion, who had not a scintilla of political influence, nor had they —at this time—any significant economic power.

How did Ezekiel plan to carry out his bold program? His first step, the one we are considering now, was to call the people back to the private, individual and family practice of their faith. He stressed heavily such observances as right diet, ritualistic prayers, and respect for the Lord's Day. He knew what his modern critics seem not to know, that these things are outward aids to (not substitutes for) an inward and spiritual relationship with God. When this relationship is marred, the person who has marred it must engage in self-examination, repentance, and the rededication of his individual life to God.

Today some Christians, who are rightly concerned about the complex issues that confront us, are openly belittling the importance of Christian practice. They seem to consider worship a personal idiosyncrasy that probably does little harm, except as it keeps a person from his really important

Christian duty out manning the barricades. No one who studies Ezekiel will belittle political activity. But surely the student must also see that underlying and guiding our activity must be the private, individual relationship with God. And this was first in Ezekiel's program for society. I append a small pragmatic footnote. Ezekiel's program worked.

EZEKIEL'S STRENGTH

Here is a young minister called by God to preach a message of repentance to people who do not want to listen. The Lord warns him of briers, thorns, and scorpions, that is, sullen hostility, rejection of the message and the messenger who delivers it, and perhaps physical danger. He will have few friends and little earthly support. Is his life therefore to be devoid of the consolation that is part of our faith? Far from that.

In the vision a Hand extends a scroll to Ezekiel. This "Hand," sometimes called the Spirit (or breath) of God, dominates the ensuing prophecy. As symbolism goes in Ezekiel, that of the scroll is clear: it represents the Holy Bible. Among the Hebrews a biblical scroll comprised many sheets of parchment sewed together to form a continuous sheet about eight or ten inches wide and twenty or thirty feet long, which was wrapped about two wooden spindles; so that the reader could roll the pages onto one as he unrolled them from the other. Such a scroll would bear a title, and so, "there were written on it words of lamentation and mourning and woe."

We do not know with any assurance how much of the Holy Bible was in existence at the time. Critics are battling loudly about the process of composition, and they have discovered, or perhaps invented, a host of editors who revised what the fathers handed down. But when this has been said, Ezekiel had a significant part of the written depository of faith that today we call the Holy Bible. He made a unique contribution to the Scripture by enriching a treasury already in existence, as others were to enrich Ezekiel's thoughts.

Ezekiel is commanded to eat the scroll, which is not difficult to do in a vision. After he begins to assimilate it, he discovers that despite the forbidding title the scroll is "as sweet as honey." The vision applies to that part of Scripture which Ezekiel himself wrote, the sweetness of which does not become apparent until you have chewed it quite thoroughly. Likewise it applies to those parts of the Bible written before Ezekiel's time and to those written after. The message of consolation, "sweet as honey" is there, but it does not become yours until you have taken into yourself the other message: your personal responsibility to Almighty God.

The Bible presents a tough, realistic picture of human weakness and divine strength. Can you find in ancient time any other writing that describes with such appalling frankness the weakness of great men? Abraham was a liar, Isaac a cheat, and Jacob a fool; and our faith looks to them as the earthly founders. But that is not the whole story. God touched these three weak men, and made them great. Then why is the story of their failings recounted with such grim detail? Precisely because all of us are weak. All of us need divine help. The Bible points to our weakness by describing people long dead. And the same Bible points to our only Help.

The one completely obvious doctrine in Christian faith is that man has sinned. Yet it is precisely this doctrine that modern man most enthusiastically rejects. Why bother about forgiveness of sin, if what people used to call sin is just a series of conditioned responses to environment (or an unfortunate heredity, or ductless glands functioning improperly, or repressions and inhibitions taking an anti-social outlet) ?

The Bible recognizes that some people are sick, and therefore are not morally responsible. In those days the sickness was called demon possession: a force beyond the individual's control governed his actions. Today we describe the same symptoms using different names. We toss these names about with such assurance that sometimes we credit them for our actions, and not ourselves. It is easier to blame an inhibition or a conditioned response or an inferiority complex for my mistakes than to accept personal responsibility for them, and confess them to God. Obviously, no one could be expected to repent for an inferiority complex, any more than for measles. So we go, evading responsibility for our acts, and wondering why God doesn't put the world to rights. He wants to. Through you.

The first step in putting the world to rights is to put yourself right. And the first step is to recognize where you have been wrong, and to do something about that. It has been said, I do not know who said it, "If you would reform the world, first reform yourself. Then you will be sure there is one less rascal in it."

Am I a rascal? Many people in the world are far worse than I. That is what the Hebrew exiles said to Ezekiel. But there is one person for whose life I am uniquely responsible. Is that person measuring up to the full stature of which he is capable with God's help? If not, that person ought to repent. This is the message of Ezekiel. This same message runs all through the Bible. People do not like the message. They never have and they probably never will. Assimilating this message is the necessary prelude to discovering the sweetness of our faith.

Over a dangerous reef the Coast Guard anchors a large buoy with a light that blinks by night and a bell that tolls with every wave. The buoy is placed there not to deprive the mariner of any freedom, but to show him the way to freedom. So the mourning and lamentation and woe that fill the Bible are placed there for our benefit.

The Bible holds high standards for human conduct. Indeed we are told on one occasion, "You...must be perfect, as your heavenly Father is perfect." It would be difficult to raise the standard any higher. We want a relaxed, easygoing moral code that makes no strenuous demands on us, and a genial grand-father in heaven who will smile upon our many shortcomings. Instead the Bible erects a standard so high that we can attain it only with divine help. Many people, understandably, reject the standard. I have not heard the term "lamentation and mourning and woe" applied to Christian morality, but scarcely a week passes without my hearing about "blue-nosed, narrow kill-joys" or something of that sort. Ezekiel was no spreader of fatuous cheer when he called his people to repent, yet it was he who led the way to the victory for which they longed.

What shall we look at? the lamentation, mourning and woe? or the sweetness like that of honey? When I start thinking about the happiest people I know, it never crosses my mind to think of those who live for their own pleasure. I know several, and I pity them. The happy people of my acquaintance have accepted heavy responsibility—be it raising a family or directing a giant corporation—and are discharging their responsibility in the light of their faith. And of them all, the happiest are the missionaries who live under conditions that would drive their critics insane. A century ago missionaries expected to find tigers sauntering through the living room, or wondered if they would provide somebody's supper tomorrow night. Most missionaries today live in crowded cities, surrounded by tensions that make cannibals look warmhearted and tigers gentle. They breathe an atmosphere of suspicion and sometimes open hatred. Physical danger is commonplace; many of their brothers and sisters have been killed in the course of duty. Yet they have a joy in their hearts that the world did not give and the world cannot take away. They have accepted the stern message of the Bible, with its call for personal responsibility to Almighty God under all circumstances, and they have learned what Ezekiel knew, that the life of disciplined faith is actually the happiest man can know.

Ezekiel was sent to proclaim the message that wherever you are, in the valley of the shadow or on the sunny highlands, it is your duty to live your faith. When you have failed, it is your duty to repent and get back to the right relationship with God, so that you can be the agent through whom His light will transform and redeem the world.

[The Lord] said to me, "Son of man, go, get you to the house of Israel, and speak with my words to them. For you are ... sent ... to the house of Israel—not to many peoples of foreign speech and a hard language, whose words you cannot understand. Surely, if I sent you to such, they would listen to you. But the house of Israel will not listen to you; for they are not willing to listen to me: because all the house of Israel are of a hard forehead and of a stubborn heart. Behold, I have made your face hard against their faces, and your forehead hard against their foreheads. Like adamant harder than flint have I made your forehead; fear them not, nor be dismayed at their looks, for they are a rebellious house.... And go, get you to the exiles, to your people, and say to them, 'Thus says the Lord God'; whether they hear or refuse to hear."

Then the Spirit lifted me up, and ... I heard behind me the voice of a great earthquake, saying, "Blessed be the glory of the Lord from its place."[1] It was the sound of the wings of the living creatures as they touched one another, and the sound of the wheels beside them.... The Spirit ... took me away, and I went in bitterness in the heat of my spirit, the Hand of the Lord being strong upon me; and I came to the exiles at Telabib, who dwelt by the river Chebar. And I sat there overwhelmed among them seven days.

And at the end of the seven days, the word of the Lord came to me: "Son of man, I have made you a watchman for the house of Israel; whenever you hear a word from my mouth, you shall give them warning from me. If I say to the wicked, 'You shall surely die,' and you give him no warning ... that wicked man shall die in his iniquity; but his blood I will require at your hand. But if you warn the wicked, and he does not turn from his wickedness ... he shall die in his iniquity; but you will have saved your life. Again, if a righteous man turns from his righteousness and commits iniquity ... he shall die; because you have not warned him ... but his blood I will require at your hand. Nevertheless if you warn the righteous man not to sin, and he does not sin, he shall surely live, because he took warning; and you will have saved your life."

And the Hand of the Lord was there upon me; and he said to me, "Arise, go forth into the plain, and there I will speak with you." So I arose and went forth into the plain; and, lo, the glory of the Lord stood there, like the glory which I had seen by the river Chebar; and I fell on my face. But the Spirit entered into me, and set me upon my feet; and he ... said ... "Go, shut yourself within your house. And ... behold, cords will be placed upon you, and you shall be bound with them, so that you cannot go out

---

[1] Adapted from the Authorized Version.

among the people; and I will make your tongue cleave to the roof of your mouth, so that you shall be dumb and unable to reprove them; for they are a rebellious house. But when I speak with you, I will open your mouth, and you shall say to them, 'Thus says the Lord God'; he that will hear, let him hear; and he that will refuse to hear, let him refuse."

THE HAND OF GOD AND
YOUR HANDS
Ezekiel 3:4-27

A minister is ordained today by the laying on of hands. This act is our modern symbol for the mystery that took place when God laid His "Hand" upon Ezekiel and made him a prophet. Ezekiel knew, from the moment of his call, that he was no longer his own agent, but God's agent. The minister today likewise is ordained to be God's agent on earth. Twenty-four centuries ago, our heavenly Father warned Ezekiel that we who represent Him must expect deafness and opposition.

Ezekiel will never rest content when his prophecy enables you to think about another person's responsibility. It's you he's interested in. What happened when you were baptized? Hands were laid on you. Did this act have meaning. Or was it just a religious gesture? We Protestants hold that every Christian in baptism is ordained a priest of God. We priests have many functions within the Church. Some lay bricks, some rock cradles, some teach school, and some break the sacramental bread. But all of us are called to be God's agents. Jesus said, "Let your light so shine before men, that they may see your good works and give glory to your Father who is in heaven." The remark was not addressed solely to the clergy.

God commissioned Ezekiel to be a prophet. He ordained me to be a minister. He baptized you to be a Christian. We three have different responsibilities within the plan of salvation, just as the helmsman, the steward, and the engineer on a ship have different duties, but they contribute their

individual skills to the common task, and they face the storms
together.

THE HAND OF GOD

In Ezekiel two words, "Hand" and "Spirit" have the same
meaning, for which, unhappily, we have retained only the
latter in English. Both represent the mystery of God-at-
work-in-the-world that we Christians name the Holy Spirit
or Holy Ghost. Ezekiel employed bold figures of speech; for
in his day "Spirit" meant "breath." God does not breathe,
nor has He the kind of hands we have. But there is a life-
principle, or spirit, in us corresponding, however imperfectly,
to the divine life-principle, or Spirit. Many compassionate
human actions are performed with the hands; so the divine
compassion may be suggested by the Hand of God.

The Spirit, who controlled and co-ordinated the different
forces of the chariot-throne, is the hero of Ezekiel's prophecy.
In all the Old Testament you will find no more significant
words about the Holy Spirit than Ezekiel's, except in Psalm
139. Here the prophet tells us something that we are ever
willing to forget: "The Spirit lifted me up and took me
away, and I went in bitterness in the heat of my spirit, the
Hand of the Lord being strong upon me."

Ezekiel has recognized the Hand of God in his moment
of exaltation. This requires little discernment. Almost anybody, when things are going well in his own life, concedes
that God is in heaven and the world is getting along somehow. Ezekiel's peculiar talent is his ability to see that the
Spirit of God is still at work when everything is going wrong
in time of "bitterness."

Most of us have known at least a few intimations of divine
glory, when the peace of the heavens saturated our thirsty
hearts. We wish that spiritual life could be like that all the
time. It isn't.

When Moses saw the burning bush, the Lord commanded
him to put off his shoes; for he stood upon holy ground.
But the Lord did not keep him there. Moses had to put the
shoes back on, and return to the land from which he was
a fugitive. Jesus prayed in the desert. After He had been
there six weeks, He came face to face with the most cruel

temptation He had yet known. Three disciples ascended the Mount with their Lord. They wanted to stay in the place of exaltation and build a chapel. Instead Christ led them down to face a human need. Had God deserted Moses when He sent him back to Egypt? Did the heavenly Father forget about Jesus during the temptation? Was the Savior mistaken in leading His followers from the Mountain to the place of cruel need? Scarcely. In each case the essential message is exactly what Ezekiel is saying: God, who is with you in the glory of your faith, is likewise with you in the drudgery.

THE WORK OF A PASTOR

God called Ezekiel to serve as pastor to a lonely, frightened group of exiles. Ezekiel does not apply the word pastor to himself, but this word in modern English best fits the job-description—if you will forgive the term—that Ezekiel receives from the Lord. We would say that Ezekiel was not ideally equipped for his task. He had powerful intellectual gifts, but what we call serious personality defects. Sometimes he succeeded in frightening people, for the moment, more than he helped them. Never has a man lived who knew less about the power of positive thinking than did Ezekiel during the early years of his ministry.

Not long ago a Roman Catholic priest said to me, "It used to be that a priest was judged by his piety, a rabbi was judged by his scholarship, and a Protestant minister by his preaching ability. Now everybody asks about any of us three, 'Is he a good Joe?'" Ezekiel was not a good Joe. Among the huddled exiles were three men who, from our viewpoint, were better equipped than Ezekiel for the burden God laid on his shoulders. Their names were Ahab, Zedekiah, and Shemaiah, and we shall think about them in more detail when we get to the chapter on false prophets. They were good Joes. They had the warmth and color that Ezekiel lacked. But they misrepresented the Lord, while Ezekiel faithfully proclaimed His will. Ezekiel did not have their gifts of personality and charm, but he served God to the full with the gifts the Lord had entrusted to him. If the Church must wait for perfect volunteers to do the Lord's work, we must wait forever. Ezekiel had his limitations, but he gave himself completely to do God's work as well as he could in the place where he was.

Now Ezekiel is sitting in his home. Thoughts of glory and of failure tangle in his mind. The political institutions of Israel have failed, and he is in exile. With growing horror, he sees that the failure must be compounded, that Jerusalem will fall, and that he must be the messenger to carry this unwanted news to his people. But just as he is about to be crushed by the impending tragedy, he recalls again the overwhelming glory that he has seen in his vision. He recognizes that his faith is more than an individual luxury to carry him through the rough days ahead. His faith gives him responsibility to convey both the doom and the glory to his fellow exiles. It is not enough for him to hoe the onions faithfully and to say his prayers on the Lord's day, he must be a watchman for his people. His term watchman and our term pastor, which means shepherd, are both figures of speech. The same responsibility underlies both.

High watch-towers stood at measured intervals along the massive walls of Babylon. When the exiles went into the city on their errands they could see the watchmen up in their towers, watching. When the exiles had gone back to their homes and the land lay dark about them, they knew that the sentinels still were at their post of duty, still watching. When a storm cloud blinded the land and others hid their faces, the watchmen remained on duty. When the rain beat down upon them, or the cruel summer sun, when their eyes ached for sleep or their throats burned with thirst, the watchmen stayed on guard in the tower and watched. The similarity to a pastor's task is easy to see. A pastor must know what is going on in the world.

The watchman was not a passive observer. When he saw something that ought not to be he called out a warning. Nobody wants to hear the watchman. Everybody wants him to keep silent; for he cries trouble and sorrow. If a fire breaks out in District Twelve, the watchman must report it immediately. If there is a riot in the market, the watchman must give the alarm. He must keep an eye on each dust-cloud in the far distance. Most of them mark camel-caravans plodding wearily along, bearing merchandise to or from the city. But one dust-cloud may be stirred up by marauders from the desert.

Whenever things go wrong, it is the watchman's duty to report. Nobody likes his report. Sometimes people condemn the bearer for the news he brings. Ivan the Terrible used to keep a great spear beside his throne. When a messenger brought word that disturbed him, he would plunge the spear through the messenger's body. Nobody objects if the pastor is a thoughtful observer of current events, but when he sounds the alarm, the people warned have been known to show signs of irritation with the one who delivered the warning.

Ezekiel sees the spiritual watchman's duty from a double perspective. First, and obviously, he must speak to the people, warning them of their collective sin. This is not an easy task, as everyone knows who has ever tried it. But God gave to Ezekiel another task that is much, much harder. Not only must he speak to the people, he must speak to the individual person. It is one thing, and a necessary, important thing, for the pastor to warn the congregation about the dangers of greed, for example. But I, at least, find it immeasurably harder to say to a particular person, "You are paying miserable wages." Ezekiel accepted this harder task.

The Son of Man describes four individuals and the watchman's relation to each. These are not flesh-and-blood people. Human behavior seldom comes in total contrasts of good and evil. Several noted racketeers have been devoted husbands and fathers, and several noted philanthropists have failed miserably in this department. Human conduct was just as complex in Ezekiel's day as in ours. But to illustrate a point he can picture a righteous man who is righteous all the way through, an evil man who is evil all the way through, and an evil man who fools the public.

The first illustration shows an evil man whom the watchman fails to warn, and who dies in his sin. The Lord says sternly to the watchman, "His blood I will require at your hand." If, while reading his prophecy, you decide that Ezekiel was rough on his contemporaries, you should appreciate that he had the same unsparing attitude toward himself. The second illustration shows the prophet warning a man who will not heed. Since the watchman has done his duty, he is guiltless of the spiritual death that follows.

The analysis of a watchman's duty makes uncomfortable reading for a pastor today. Social conditions have changed, naturally, but the stresses and strains that Ezekiel and the false prophets knew are still with us. The third illustration shows one of a pastor's most baffling duties, that of dealing with a person whose outward actions are correct, and all the while he is sliding from the faith until in a horrible manner he denies the Lord altogether. The watchman has failed to warn; he is guilty of the other person's spiritual death. The final illustration shows the ideal. A person is faithful to God. The watchman helps him to practice his faith. And so, spiritually, both live.

THE WORK OF A CANDLESTICK MAKER

God calls different kinds of people to different kinds of work. Only a few are called to serve Him by giving their full time to the multiple tasks of the organized Church. Yet God calls every Christian to a Christian vocation. Your work, as doctor, lawyer, merchant, or chief is your ministry to God. And what Ezekiel says about his work applies just as much to yours. Our work is all dealing with people. We call them customers or suppliers or union representatives. Sometimes, to be sure, we call them pests. Each is a person, made in the image of God, created to enter eternal blessedness, and having difficulties along the way. Your task is to help him.

In modern life our contact with people sometimes is indirect. And how about Ezekiel's, when he was out hoeing the onion patch? During the early years of his ministry he did not influence large numbers. Instead, he influenced a few so deeply that they changed world history. One of the most influential Christians I have ever known is an automobile mechanic. His friends seldom see much more of him than his feet sticking out from under a car. Occasionally he comes up for air, and they see his face, marked with little greasy smudges. He never has much to say. God did not give him the gift of eloquence. But he expresses an air of integrity to everyone with whom he deals. One day he said to me, "Every time I work on a car, I know that I'm taking the life of one of God's children in my hands." His customers, his suppliers, and his competitors all realize that he is a man who knows Christ, and who practices his faith with every twist of the wrench. It is not easy for an automobile mechanic to be such a person that those around him will know God through him. It was not easy for Ezekiel. It is not easy for your pastor. It is not easy for you. But this is the task to which God has called you.

CORDS AND DUMBNESS

As his ministry began, Ezekiel foresaw briers, thorns, scorpions, cords and dumbness. For reasons unknown to me, biblical students have tried to take the cords and the dumbness literally, while they correctly understood that the thorns and scorpions are symbolic. Nobody thinks that Ezekiel really sat on scorpions. Neither was he literally tied up with strings, and he went on talking—to people who would not listen. These are figures of speech for the difficulties a representative of God must expect. The briers and thorns and scorpions represent the unpleasantness, discouragement, and sometimes physical danger of living and teaching a Gospel that others reject. For example, in our turbulent twentieth century, Christians have lost their lives or have been permanently crippled because they dared to say out loud that our cultural patterns regarding the Negro and the white man have not been in accord with God's will.

Scorpions continue scuttling about the Church. But the cords and the dumbness are even more serious. These are the limitations within which faith must work. We proclaim a Gospel that will transform people, if they will accept it. "If" is a short word that carries a long train of consequence. The cords mean that you cannot make me accept the Gospel. The dumbness means that you cannot even make me listen, if I will not. But it remains your responsibility to proclaim your faith, through the personality God entrusted to you, to the people with whom you have natural, normal contact. Let's look at a few of the difficulties.

There is just one of me, and the world's need is so great. How true. And so, a good many people have decided, I shall do nothing. There was only one of Ezekiel, and he had far

less political influence and financial importance than you
have. But he lived completely for God, where he was, with
the talents he had. He knew that no man can save his own
soul while ignoring the souls about him. As the ensuing
prophecy illustrates graphically, some of the people around
Ezekiel were hard to get along with. Some of them were
busily trying to forget about God. Some would not give
Ezekiel the slightest heed. But some listened, once in a while.
Regardless, he encouraged them all to be faithful to God
where they were, and to serve Him with the talents they
had.

Far more important than the limitation of numbers is the
necessary limit of knowledge. How can I introduce Christ
to a person I don't know? You can never really know what
is going on in my mind. In his four black-or-white case
studies Ezekiel shows one who is outwardly virtuous but is
a rotter at heart. Likewise, I have known warm-hearted,
generous people who unwisely protected themselves with
a veneer of harsh attitude. How can I talk about Christ to
a stranger?

The other fellow has a long history bearing on his character today. You don't know that history, even for the
members of your own family. It has been said, with partial
accuracy, "To know all is to pardon all." It is popular and
sometimes profitable to talk about the subconscious forces
bearing on your character. These are unknown to you. Far
less are your neighbor's subconscious forces known to you.
Here is someone who is attracted or repelled by influences
that you know nothing about. How can you do or say anything to reach him at the point of moral decision? It isn't
easy. Ezekiel didn't find it so.

One more difficulty you will encounter in presenting your
Christian witness: the other person wants you to mind your
own business, not his. You cannot force your faith on anyone
without doing violence both to his personality and to your
faith. Since the world is a large place and many strange
people are in it, there have been occasions when someone
has actually done some good by buttonholing a stranger and
asking, "Are you saved?" After talking with many who have
been alienated from the Gospel by this blunderbus approach

to salvation, I would estimate that the harm exceeds the good by a proportion of about ten to one.

On the wall of the delivery room in Good Samaritan Hospital is a large sign, AT LEAST DO NO HARM. This is the first principle of medicine. Christians might take it to heart. In our zeal to save the other person we ought not to antagonize him. There is quite enough scandal in the Cross, when presented with sensitivity and intelligence, without our giving unnecessary offense by our bad manners.

It's hard to take a rational, helpful stand for Christ in the crazy mixed-up world where we live. So what's the conclusion? Sit back and do nothing? It was hard for Ezekiel to stand firm for God. He had a negative personality. But it was the only personality he had; so he served God with it. You are not called to follow the prophet in his weakness, but in his strength. He knew that it would be hard to be a watchman, but God called him to the work and he did it.

Ezekiel's message to you is threefold. First the glory of God is found wherever faith in Him exists, even by the River Chebar. Second, God is in charge of this world and He will be victorious over it. Third, your part in the final victory is to practice your faith to the utmost, where you are.

Ezekiel 6:1-10

Thus says the Lord God to the mountains, and the hills, to the ravines and the valleys: "Behold, I, even I, will bring a sword upon you, and I will destroy your high places. Your altars shall become desolate, and your incense altars shall be broken; and I will cast down your slain before your idols. And I will lay the dead bodies of the people of Israel before their idols; and I will scatter your bones round about your altars. Wherever you dwell your cities shall be waste and your high places ruined, . . . and your idols broken and destroyed, your incense altars cut down, and your works wiped out. And the slain shall fall in the midst of you, and you shall know that I am the Lord.

"Yet I will leave some of you alive. When you have among the nations some who escape the sword, and when you are scattered through the countries, then those of you who escape will remember me among the nations where they are carried captive, when I have broken their wanton heart which has departed from me, and blinded their eyes which turn wantonly after their idols; and they will be loathsome in their own sight for the evils which they have committed, for all their abominations. And they shall know that I am the Lord; I have not said in vain that I would do this evil to them."

THE HOPE THAT GROWS
FROM FAITH
Ezekiel 6:1-10

I have called *The Book of Ezekiel* the most hopeful message ever delivered. I will concede without the slightest argument that hope is not one's first or second impression upon looking into this gloomy, sometimes horrible, book. I believe that the sixth is the most dreadful chapter in the entire prophecy. It drips blood, and its pages reek with the stench of war. Yet this chapter illustrates why an intelligent man, facing sure disaster, still can live and work in hope.

Ezekiel is contemporary. Our morning papers, day after day, report just what Ezekiel reports: war and rumors of war, riot, insurrection, and rebellion. Political analysts pick up each crisis and explore its inner and outer significance, just as Ezekiel did. The analysts today finish leaving us with a feeling of dread. But when Ezekiel finished his study of the human situation, he left to all generations a legacy of hope.

WHAT DO WE MEAN BY HOPE?

Hope is a desire, joined with an expectation that the thing desired will be, or can be, gained. A hope is a feeling. There has been a heavy emphasis on religious feeling in modern times, and this emphasis has done great mischief. The stress goes back to Schleiermacher, who claimed that the essence of religion is a feeling of creaturely dependence. From his keen introspective analysis has followed a long, slow process of degeneration, until today many believe that religion is primarily concerned with feeling.

Among the dubious, the common cliche is, "I can feel

just as religious out in the woods as I can in Church." And
this, they hope, ends the matter. Among devout Christians,
the complaint is frequent: "But I don't *feel* anything when
I pray." So much is this heard that Arthur John Gossip
writes, near the beginning of his valuable study, *In the
Secret Place of the Most High:*

> The first lesson the masters in devotion keep impressing on
> us is that we must outgrow the habit of assessing the value
> of a time of prayer by the sensible fervours and the glow
> at the heart which it awakens in us ... We must ... learn to
> trust Him in the dark; to walk by faith, not sight; to build
> upon His word and promise, and not on our own feelings.

Jesus tells us what to believe. He tells us what to do. But
He never tells us how to feel. This, after all, is beyond our
conscious control. You can say to yourself, "I will be buoyant,
hopeful, and optimistic." But that won't make you buoyant,
hopeful, and optimistic. Your feelings are an involuntary
response to events, colored by the experiences, remembered
or forgotten, you bring to these events.

A sensible person cannot respond to the hydrogen bomb,
Communist subversion, the population explosion, or biological warfare with any hopeful feelings. Yet today's happen-
ings are no more destructive to hope than those in Ezekiel's
time. Analyzing events alone would have left Ezekiel despairing and cynical, just like his contemporaries, and ours. But
Ezekiel examined events as illumined by his experience of
the living God. He looked beyond the events and their necessarily tragic outcome to God's final victory. He brought the
light of faith to bear upon the darkness of history, and
learned to hope.

In 1861 a young woman, Julia Ward Howe, went with
some friends to a military review near Washington. Much
later, she described the thoughts that went running through
her mind—thoughts that have been shared by countless millions in every dangerous age— "You would be glad to serve,
but you cannot help anyone; you have nothing to give, and
there is nothing for you to do." As the party was returning
from the review, marching troops surounded and blocked
their carriage. The party began singing various popular songs,
including *John Brown's Body*. The soldiers took up the

song, shouting its words—not always elegant—as they marched back to their bivouac areas.

Mrs. Howe's pastor, the Reverend James Freeman Clarke, was among the party. He suggested that it was a pity to waste such a glorious tune on such shabby words, and suggested that she correct the lack. The next morning shortly before dawn, she wakened, with words running through her mind. She rose, not daring to light a candle lest she rouse the baby, and wrote her thoughts about the Civil War.

To read some contemporary historians, one would gather that there was nothing much to the Civil War but corruption, graft, inefficiency, disease, cruelty, and stupidity. These things were all there, in outsize quantities, but Mrs. Howe had the faith that taught her to look deeper. She saw the glory, and she wrote *The Battle Hymn of the Republic*, with imagery straight from Ezekiel (via *The Revelation.*) Her faith had taught her to hope. It did not teach her to ignore what is base and horrible, but to see the glory. It is a rare person today who looks within the storm-clouds to the shining glory. We have forgotten how to hope.

WHAT IS THE ALTERNATIVE?

What is the alternative to hope? We have an English word that means "no-hope," which I hear frequently. It comes to us from the Latin language, where hope is *sperare*. No-hope is *de-sperare*. And the English word is *despair*. Ezekiel used a completely different word to describe the attitude, naturally. But he was familiar with the thing we are talking about; he lived with it all the time. His friends and neighbors had already succumbed to despair, and he too knew moments when it seemed that God had forgotten.

What happens when people give up hope? We usually think about despair as a passive attitude. A person quits fighting, and lets life run over him like a relentless steamroller. But despair has another face that is completely different. If you watch television with any frequency, you have not failed to see the hard-drinkin', gun-slingin' *desperado*. A desperado is a bad man, who lives by violence, and cares little for the lives of those who get in his way. Why? "Desperado" is an old Spanish word meaning, "the one who has lost hope." Since he does not have hope to guide him and steady him, the desperado lives without concern for the future or for his neighbors, gratifying his desires as well as he can. He is desperate, which of course means hopeless.

Hope is not the whipped cream that may fall upon society, but the cement that binds together the other essentials for decent life.

I have said, and I will say it again, that nothing in the human situation inspires hope today. So respectable people take out their despair in respectable ways, and people who aren't turn to violence. The crime rate in our country is growing five times as fast as the rate of population growth. And, even more significant, we are coming to expect hatred and violence, both national and international.

The political situation in Ezekiel's day illustrates what I have been saying. The connection between hopelessness and passive resignation and brutal violence is no accident imposed upon us by the Latin language. It is written into the constitution of human nature. Ezekiel and his close companions were exiled. They were giving way to the passive kind of hopelessness, forgetting their long-range spiritual dreams, and cynically adjusting to a meaningless, monotonous existence, getting and spending, doing the best they could. But in Jerusalem a group of madmen was involved in the other kind of desperation. They were plotting a rebellion against King Nebuchadnezzar. Sometimes a person is in a situation where he decides that things could not possibly get worse. When he turns to desperate solutions, he usually finds that they can.

HOW DO YOU ACHIEVE HOPE?

How do you achieve hope? I know several approaches, most of which don't work. A few people seem to have a built-in sunny disposition. Nothing ruffles them. Earthquake, famine and pestilence cannot dim the brightness of their outlook. In its extreme form this attitude is called *euphoria,* a symptom of serious mental illness. I do not know how the eternal viewers-with-cheer achieve their state of bliss. I suspect it has something to do with their blood-chemistry, which doesn't help the rest of us a bit. Ezekiel was not among the irritating optimists, and yet it was he who taught his fellow-exiles, and us, to hope in the midst of horror.

You can play an elaborate game of blind-man's-buff with yourself, trying to kid yourself that things probably aren't so bad as they seem to be. Much can be said in favor of this attitude. Most of us worry far more about trifles than we ought. Most of us manufacture troubles where there are none. A right attitude can evaporate imaginary difficulties, and can bring genuine difficulties into their true proportional size. Yet life also contains difficulties that no amount of positive thinking will clear away.

When I was in the fourth grade, a classmate named Marjorie—I have forgotten her last name—reviewed the book *Pollyanna.* As she reported the story, Pollyanna was a girl who went through life looking upon the bright side and ignoring the dark. She was determinedly cheerful all the time, and sure enough things worked out, sooner or later. I was widely known as the cynic of the fourth grade, and I remarked to my colleague Billy Whitelaw that Pollyanna sounded stupid. I have never read the book. Perhaps Marjorie's presentation has steered me away from an important contribution to thought. But I have met people who refuse to face reality in their frantic pursuit of happiness. That way lies not hope but madness.

Critics have said many harsh things about Ezekiel, but none has ever said that he refused to face the unpleasant facts. He is almost brutal in his insistence that we examine every unpleasantness in every detail. The false prophets said that trouble would disappear if the exiles ignored it long enough. Ezekiel teaches us to look through the trouble to God. The false prophets cheerfully led their followers into a blind alley of despair. Ezekiel gloomily leads his into the bright light of hope.

I hesitate even to mention the chemical approach to hope. It has long been known that ethyl alcohol, taken immoderately, will produce a temporary feeling of well-being and sometimes an optimistic outlook on the future. Every adult knows that the long-term results can be only disastrous. Modern science has produced another chemical aid, of immeasurable value to the physician, that is being widely abused today. The inordinate sale of tranquillizers leads me to conclude that some, at least, who are Christian are using such drugs unwisely, with demonstrated dangers to their health.

In the United States we usually try to shift the environment around until it fits our desires. We have been more successful at environment-moulding than have most people. We have irrigated deserts and drained swamps. We have torn down slums and built red-brick apartment houses in their place. We have set up a form of government that offers marvelous possibilities of freedom and justice for all. We have created the most powerful defensive force in human history. We have lengthened the span of life. We have made education available to almost everybody. And the question rises: Are we a hopeful people? We do not impress others that way. Hope is not ringing through our political and social pronouncements.

Without belittling any needed social change, we ought to realize that controlling the environment is not enough. Ezekiel might help us to realize it. Here is a man who has no ability to control anything. He is a political pawn in a gigantic chess game. People and forces totally unconcerned about him as an individual person control his daily actions, yet he has something the environment-molders lack. He has hope.

The most familiar words about hope, to the contemporary Christian, are those spoken by Paul, "Now abideth faith, hope, charity, these three; but the greatest of these is charity." Yet in our thinking about these words we usually overlook hope. Faith means the intellectual acceptance of some ideas about God as revealed through Jesus Christ, coupled with a commitment of self, not so much to the ideas as to God. Charity is the desire that good may come to a person and putting the desire into action when possible. Faith is the motive power, and charity is the thing put into motion. Faith is the gasoline and charity is the engine. Between the gasoline and the engine is an inconspicuous copper tube. We don't pay much attention to it, unless it develops a leak or gets clogged. Hope is something like that. Certainly it is not the earthly end-product of Christianity; that is charity.

Certainly it is not the motive power; that is faith. But without hope there is precious little charity. And without hope faith soon withers into the bored acceptance of a few propositions about God.

How do you develop hope? The best way is to forget about hope and to work on faith and charity. The love of God is the creator and the sustainer of hope.

The love of God has two meanings. It means that God loves you, and that you love God. His love for you is constant and unchanging, you could not improve it if you wanted to. Your love for Him changes from time to time. You cannot make yourself love God, but you can seek His company, or you can shun Him. Nobody else can do this for you. You can wallow in the murk where it is almost impossible to see that the light is shining. You can busy yourself with the failings of your neighbors. You can revel in the pornography that festers on the bookstalls. Or you can think about "whatsoever things are true, whatsoever things are honest, whatsoever things are just, whatsoever things are pure, whatsoever things are lovely, whatsoever things are of good report."

As a Christian, you certainly ought to keep up with what is going on in the world. But you can ask yourself a question, the answer to which might explain the presence or absence of hope in your heart. How much time do I spend informing myself about the news of today, and how much time do I give to thinking about eternity? If I spend an hour with the newspaper and five minutes with the Bible, it isn't surprising if the forces of darkness look twelve times as strong as the forces of light.

Faith is never a private luxury, designed to fill our hearts with pretty sentiments. The secular world has a deserved contempt for that kind of faith. Christian faith must be concerned with human needs. Christian faith must reach beyond self, into the heartache of society. Christian faith must be concerned about poverty, ignorance, and disease. Christian faith must be concerned about good or bad government. A Christian must care about the conditions that affect people because the people affected are his brothers. A Christian has many brothers who are well-washed, attractive, intelligent, and polite, who have deep hungers that no material prosperity can fill. A Christian likewise has brothers who are not at all attractive. Toward both, the Christian's attitude is charity.

I talk with many people in the course of a week about many issues. I talk with people on every level of the economic or educational scale. In regard to this matter of hope that we are now discussing, it doesn't seem to me to make the slightest difference how rich or how poor a person may be, how well or how little educated. The people who are living their faith in charity seem to me to have hope—coupled with full awareness of the difficulties and dangers. And the others don't.

THE SPECIFIC OF EZEKIEL'S HOPE

Ezekiel was an exile, in the flat, monotonous plains of Babylon. If I may speak quite personally, among the few strong dislikes I have for life in coastal Florida is the flat landscape. Until I came here, hills were a part of my daily life. I never realized how much they meant to me until I was separated from them. Take my feelings and multiply them by a hundred, and you will have a faint suggestion of Ezekiel's feelings. He missed the hills he had known in boyhood. But this was more than the normal, healthy attachment of a man to his native soil. The low mountains were silent reminders of God's promise to Abraham. Hebrew faith was linked to the Palestinian hills.

We cannot know the pain that separation from his country brought to Ezekiel. Far less can we know the anguish it brought him to prophesy that foreign troops would invade the homeland and make desolate the hills. The prediction was fulfilled in grisly detail, and the fulfillment was worse than reading about it. Yet, in making the prediction, Ezekiel says something that we must stop to examine.

> Thus says the Lord God to the mountains and the hills, to the ravines and the valleys: "Behold, I, even I, will bring a sword upon you."

The thought is not widely accepted today among Christians, whose usual expression about any disaster is, "I don't believe that God had anything to do with this."

Now we go back to Ezekiel's original vision. Here he has

proof, the silent, incommunicable proof of faith, that God is. The account of the vision expresses God's irresistible power, as the chariot-throne moves "straight forward." At the same moment it expresses His concern for His people, chiefly through the symbolism of eyes, hands, and a voice. As we all know, it is one thing to say in the comfort of your easy chair that God is omnipotent. It is quite another thing, when the stink of battle is in your nostrils, and you are losing the war, to proclaim that God is almighty, and that God is love. Yet this is what we Christians are called upon to say with our lives all the time.

Faith means trust in God beyond the limits of vision, but faith is not blind. Here Ezekiel introduces a thought that is to become a motif in his prophecy: the *remnant*. After prophesying slaughter and destruction, he says to the complacent people in Jerusalem, "Those of you who escape will remember me among the nations where they are carried captive." In conjunction with this thought, he introduces a phrase that ties the whole prophecy together: "You shall know that I am the Lord." In the ensuing message the phrase occurs with this wording fifty-four times and with an expanded wording eighteen times more.

The specific form of Ezekiel's hope is that almighty God (the adjective is not a mere honorific) is working through the impending destruction, and that He will save a remnant of the faithful, through whom He will reveal Himself to the world. Others than Ezekiel developed this last thought to the fullest glory.

We cannot bask in the thought of God's ultimate triumph without thinking about the faithful who died when Jerusalem fell. They knew starvation during the protracted siege. They buried their children who succumbed to disease. They manned the ramparts when they were too weak to stand. They knew hunger and horror and fear. Was it any consolation to them that the faith would survive? That depends upon what faith means to a person.

Those in Jerusalem who lived their faith are living with God today in eternity. We see on earth a small but important part of life. In our better moments we know that, when finally we stand beside our Father and look back at human history from the heavenly perspective, we shall thank God for the sufferings we knew. The righteous in Jerusalem who fell during one crucial phase of the battle for God's triumph did not lose their lives, they gave them in order that others might live. Centuries after their time, the other Son of Man expressed it: "He who loses his life for my sake will find it."

And the remnant who were dragged off to captivity — what of them? We know that during the exile the faith, instead of guttering out, burst into its greatest intensity of light. Most of the remnant did not live to see the glory that was to develop, let alone God's final triumph on earth.

> These all died in faith, not having received what was promised, but having seen it and greeted it from afar, and having acknowledged that they were strangers and exiles on the earth.
> Hebrews 11:13

Aren't we in exactly the same position? We have at least outgrown the fatuous optimism of a generation ago, that the world will keep on improving until finally we will have pulled ourselves into the Kingdom by our own valiant effort. Today the hydrogen bomb forces us back to Ezekiel's standing ground: God is almighty; God works through the disasters of history; God will triumph. It follows: here and now I am responsible to live and work for His triumph. My life counts.

We are Christians. We are not to be conformed to this world, which ought to mean that faith carries our thoughts beyond visible causes and effects. We have been touched by the Holy Spirit — as Ezekiel was touched. This fact ought to color our attitudes toward the future.

Take the central section of the Apostles' Creed, where we affirm of our Savior:

> He was crucified, dead, and buried. He descended into hell. The third day he rose again from the dead. He ascended into heaven. From thence he shall come again to judge the quick and the dead.

"From thence." From where? From heaven, obviously. But, more important to our present thought, from hell, from the tomb, from the Cross, from the mock-trial, from denial, from desertion, from betrayal. These are the means by which the eternal Christ wins His victory.

What shall we say then to these things? Jesus claims, "Behold I make all things new." We might let Him work on our attitude toward current history, which badly needs renewing. We must learn from above where to focus our thoughts. If we are Christians we must look at everything in the light of the Cross. When our thoughts are conformed to this world, we look at the madhouse and give up in despair. When our minds are renewed by the transforming power of Christ, we see exactly the same needs in the world about us, which provide us with abundant opportunity to practice the charity that faith develops. We open our eyes to the light shining within the storm clouds, and we hope.

Ezekiel 11:14-20

Son of man, your brethren, even your brethren, your fellow exiles, the whole house of Israel, all of them, are those of whom the inhabitants of Jerusalem have said, "They have gone far from the Lord; to us this land is given for a possession."

Therefore say, "Thus says the Lord God: 'Though I removed them far off among the nations, and though I scattered them among the countries, yet I have been a sanctuary to them for a while in the countries where they have gone."

Therefore say, "Thus says the Lord: 'I will gather you from the peoples, and assemble you out of the countries where you have been scattered, and I will give you the land of Israel. And when they come there, they will remove from it all its detestable things and all its abominations. And I will give them one heart, and put a new spirit within them; I will take the stony heart out of their flesh and give them a heart of flesh, that they may walk in my statutes and keep my ordinances and obey them; and they shall be my people, and I will be their God.' "

OUR REFUGE AND OUR FORTRESS
Ezekiel 11:14-20

THE PLIGHT OF THE EXILES

Nebuchadnezzar took the finest, strongest people among the Hebrews to be hostages in Babylon. A hostage is a political device, kept to guarantee some one's good behavior. But a hostage is likewise a person, fully supplied with human feelings. And those among whom Ezekiel worked felt that God had failed. As if this were not enough, their brothers in faith who remained in Jerusalem were vigorously severing the ties of understanding and charity with which the exiled hostages longed to be bound. The people in Jerusalem were saying about their brothers, "They have gone far from the Lord; to us this land is given for a possession."

It is hard enough to bear the reproaches of an enemy or the just reproaches of a friend, but the exiles, who at least were no worse than their brothers in Jerusalem, ached from calumny when they needed love. Jeremiah mentions fairly regular communication between Jerusalem and Babylon. Those in each community knew what those in the other were doing and saying; so the exiles knew that their brothers in faith and blood were despising and rejecting them.

Tragedy had struck the exiles. Whenever tragedy comes, someone is sure to call it punishment for sin, and sometimes, of course, it is. But we who look to God through a Cross know that often those who suffer are the best, not the worst among us, and we realize anew that, in ways inscrutible to us, God is working out His purpose.

We do not know how widespread was the contemptible

71

attitude in Jerusalem. We can be sure that many kind, decent people did not share it, but enough were reproaching the exiles to create scars hundreds of miles away. The attitude may be summarized: It is bad to be away from Jerusalem. The exiles are away from Jerusalem. Therefore the exiles are bad. But a worse argument — if possible — ensued. It is good to be in Jerusalem. We are in Jerusalem. Therefore we are good. It requires no skill in logic to see through the argument when it is stated that way. Naturally the perpetrators gave their shabby thoughts enough theological decor to make them sound respectable.

In the long history of religious thought, which is filled with beauty and glory, are likewise some unworthy pages, where people have baptized their own wishes as the eternal will of God. While the exiled leaders of Hebrew society still lived in Jerusalem, their inferiors secretly envied them. When Nebuchadnezzar made them hostages, the inferiors took over the places of leadership. To divert attention from their own inadequacies, they pointed scornfully at those whom they had replaced.

What the exiles needed from their brothers in faith was understanding, sympathy, and encouragement. What they received was contempt. Both groups proclaimed a faith. One group was vigorously denying it in attitude and act. The exiles were tempted to deny it by despair.

GOD CARES

The Lord sent a message to His people, the exiles, who were smarting under the snobbery of their brothers in Jerusalem. The message began: "Son of Man, your brethren, even your brethren, your fellow exiles, the whole house of Israel, all of them." In Ezekiel, where fullness of expression is commonplace, this is an unusually full statement, designed to draw our attention. That the exiles were Ezekiel's brothers, no one could doubt. But here the Lord calls them "the whole house of Israel."

Israel was the name given to Jacob, the earthly father of the sons who headed the twelve tribes that were known thenceforth as The Children of Israel, or sometimes The House of Israel. The name Israel stands collectively for the entire community of faith. To take one example from dozens, in Psalm 121 we sing: "He that keepeth Israel shall neither slumber nor sleep." Israel means not only an individual, but every individual who composes the community of faith. And here Ezekiel says, on behalf of the Lord, that the true Israel is to be found, not in Jerusalem, where the privilege of faith exists, but among the exiles, where the struggles and perils of faith are at their height.

When we Christians read about Israel, we are tempted to leave the discussion in the ancient past, where it does us not the slightest good. But our New Testament teaches us something quite different, especially in the letters to Romans and Galatians, where the Apostle Paul argues a taut, logical case, that we Christians are Israel, holding the faith delivered once to Abraham and fulfilled in Christ. Indeed, Paul concludes his letter to the Galatians with the thought: "Peace and mercy be upon all who walk by this rule, upon the Israel of God." So when we Christians read about promises made to Israel and duties required of him, we ought not to think about someone else, however important the other person may have been in the development of our faith. We ought to think about ourselves. Here in Ezekiel the message is clearcut. The outward institutions of faith are important only as they are vehicles of faith itself. Faith can survive without the outward and visible institutions. And where faith is, there is Israel.

The way of faith may be rocky and uphill all the way. Ezekiel and the other Son of Man tell us this a thousand times. As Jesus departed from the soldiers He was sending into battle, where individually they would be defeated, He promised them: "Lo, I am with you alway, even unto the end of the world." The end of the world is certainly not the South Pole or any other almost inaccessible place, nor should we think of it exclusively as the end of human history — which appears to be rushing upon us. We can likewise recognize the end of the world as the all-too-accessible depth of despair into which we so readily enter.

Ezekiel's message of hope is much the same as Jesus'. He was talking with friends who were geographically far from the place they longed to be. They knew ties of kinship and affection and religious faith with their brothers in Jerusalem, yet the brothers were hacking away at these ties with the blunt axe of snobbery. And the Lord said about the exiles, through Ezekiel:

> Though I removed them far off among the nations, and though I scattered them among the countries, yet I have been a sanctuary to them for a while in the countries where they have gone.

The translation in the Authorized Version is more beautiful, if perhaps less accurate, "I will be to them as a little sanctuary." It is both a statement of fact and a promise for the future.

What is a sanctuary? The Hebrew is *miqdosh,* which comes from the key word to the Old Testament, *qadosh,* or "holy." I believe that if you could fully understand the meaning of "holy" you could understand the Old Testament, just as you could understand the New by fully appreciating all the meanings wrapped together in the word "grace." A *miqdosh* is a holy place, a location where man is more conscious of God's universal presence than he is normally. All their lives the exiles had considered the Temple as the sanctuary, as had their fathers centuries before them. Their thoughts, their attitudes, their entire life centered upon the sacrifices offered on the high altar which stood before the Temple on the holy mountain. This was their sanctuary.

Since Ezekiel devotes eight chapters of his prophecy to describing the Temple of the future, we may take it for granted that he recognized the psychological importance of having a place to worship. He knew that God is everywhere, as he told us in describing his initial vision. And yet he realized that our human weakness is strengthened immeasurably if we make a practice of worshiping Him somewhere. He believed in the visible institutions of faith, but he taught that God Himself is above and beyond all visible institutions. And if, in the providence of God, the Temple is destroyed, God Himself will be the sanctuary. Faith will be possible, even in Babylon.

Sanctuary had a secondary meaning, which today is primary for us who speak English. In the first Book of Kings we read of two instances where an accused man went to the tabernacle and grasped the horns of the altar. While he was there, the police were unwilling to take him. The sanctuary was a place of asylum, a spiritual fortress.

When God declares Himself the sanctuary, He says that His presence is more than any visible institution. Where faith exists, there is the true Israel, and there is the Temple that really matters, not so much the place as the fact of worship. Where the reality of worship takes place is spiritual safety.

Jerusalem was besieged and conquered. The visible Temple was destroyed. Many residents in Jerusalem, who had brazenly despised the exiles, perished during the siege. Many more were exiled to Babylon. Some escaped to Egypt and other countries. And God kept His promise. He was a sanctuary — in every sense of the term — to Israel.

Visible institutions are important. During the exile the Hebrews developed a visible institution other than the Temple. No longer could they offer their sacrifices upon the altar; for they were several months' journey from the holy mountain, and the altar lay in ruins. But they gathered together, at first in one another's homes, for prayer and instruction in the Holy Scripture. And gradually they developed a new institution, the synagogue, which continues among the Jewish people today, and in reference to Ezekiel, still is called the "little sanctuary."

By the early middle ages the Christian Church was modeled upon the pattern of the Temple, with its rigid hierarchy and its elaborate ceremonial. At the time of the Protestant Reformation, the reforming fathers turned back to the pattern of the first century Church, which was the Christian adaptation of the synagogue, with its informal structure and its emphasis upon lay participation in work and worship. Protestants have found through the past four centuries that God still is our "little sanctuary." He has kept His promise.

God still keeps His promise. Recently a friend told me about a conversation with a Swiss Red Cross worker, stationed in Northern Korea where the practice of Christianity has been dangerous for the past twenty years. The Red Cross worker, walking down a crowded street, passed a shabbily dressed workman who was humming a tune. The Swiss

gentleman was experienced enough to show no sign of interest. But he paused for a fraction of a second, ostensibly to
search for a paper in his pocket, long enough to identify the
tune as "Jesus Loves Me." The little sanctuary is in North
Korea today. The reality of worship continues, among lonely,
frightened people, who still can say, "God is our refuge and
our fortress." The sanctuary is not a building on a hilltop,
but the reality of faith in God who is where you are.

THE PRACTICE OF FAITH

Some Christians today, viewing the startling changes that
are taking place within the visible Church, are predicting
almost gleefully that the visible institution will be destroyed
and — if I understand them correctly — a new Churchless
Christianity will rise in place of the old. Since I now spend
a great deal of my time dusting ecclesiastical bric-a-brac, I
can view major changes in the Church with equanimity. If
the bric-a-brac must go, so much the better. But the idea of
long-continued faith without visible institutions is not very
good psychology, or Christianity either.

God is above all institutions. He does not need them. But
we do. So Ezekiel, who foresaw the collapse of the institutions
that had sustained his faith since boyhood, and who helped
to develop the new institution, the synagogue, to guide the
despairing faith among the exiles, looks far into the future
and foresees a new expression of faith in a visible institution
remarkably similar to the one his people had known. We
might at least recognize that hitherto the efforts toward institutionless Christianity have either become new institutions
or have fizzled out.

In predicting events that lay half a century beyond his
time, the prophet sets before us a pattern for Christian action.
Ezekiel foresees a physical return of Israel to the Promised
Land. And the first item on the agenda for the returned people is: "When they come there, they will remove from it all
its detestable things and all its abominations." He was talking
about high places and sacred groves and the altars at which
Canaanites had offered their hideous sacrifices. Now-a-days
when people talk glibly about the good that is in all religions,
they conveniently overlook many chapters of history. We

acknowledge with sorrow tragic abuses in Christian history. Take away the abuses, and you have a pure and glorious faith. Take away the abuses from the worship of Molech, and what have you left? Molech, you remember, was the deity in whose honor little children were slaughtered and burned. Or there was the female deity, Ashtarte, adored by prostitution and homosexuality. Doubtless you can find some good if you explore these ancient cults long enough, but to some of us Ezekiel's approach seems more realistic. If something is detestable and abominable, get rid of it.

It was easy to destroy an altar built in honor of a false god. A hammer and a crowbar were the preferred tools. But Ezekiel is not talking about mere physical changes on the landscape, except as they reflect new attitudes in human hearts.

Is there anything in our hearts that is abominable and detestable? Read through the Sermon on the Mount, slowly and thoughtfully. Doubtless you will be able to think of all sorts of people who ought to apply what Jesus is saying. Instead, look into a mirror. Self-examination in the presence of Christ usually discloses several obstacles to spiritual development that ought to be removed. Those of us who make a fairly systematic practice of self-examination find large obstacles of habit and attitude that cannot be torn down in half an hour — like an altar to Ashtarte — instead the process of removal takes a lifetime.

Salvation requires much heroic effort on the part of the one who is saved, but it is not a do-it-yourself program. The central question dividing Christendom today can be sharply phrased: Does salvation come from God? or does salvation come from man? This was the issue dividing the Council at Nicea in 325, not the spelling of a word. And Ezekiel, like the other human authors of Holy Scripture, after stressing to the full our need for human effort, hears the Lord saying:

> I will give them one heart, and put a new spirit within them; I will take the stony heart out of their flesh and give them a heart of flesh.

The stony heart is the attitude, "My will be done." The heart of flesh prays, "Thy will be done." Notice how quietly and subtly Ezekiel has underscored his teaching about per-

sonal responsibility to God by using the word "flesh" in two
different senses. First he uses it to mean the human body
when the spirit defies God. This body is subject to all the
limitations of creaturehood, but these are not bad, unless we
choose to make them so. After the miracle of faith has been
wrought, the same word describes a warm heart, responsive
to God's will. The aim of faith is not to escape from flesh,
but to become what flesh was created to be.

The other Son of Man, in his conversation with Nico-
demus, draws a comparison between physical birth and spiritual re-birth. The first is a divine creative act, brought about
through human agencies. Human agents influence the second,
but it, too, is a creative act of God, who will do everything
in His power to work the miracle of a new heart in you.

The people in whom God is working the miracle live in
a world filled with tensions and temptations. That is why
they need the faith, or, as Ezekiel calls it here, the heart of
flesh: "that they may walk in my statutes and keep my ordinances and obey them." God knows, and all His critics
have been swift to point out, that keeping God's ordinances
can degenerate into a mere outward observance of meaningless rules and regulations. But read through the statutes
and ordinances that were in Ezekiel's hands. They talk of
justice and mercy. They decree the golden grace of friend-
liness and hospitality. They admonish against falsehood and
impurity, while they inculcate respect, honor and loyalty.
You can divorce God's statutes from civilized life if you try
hard enough, and some have done so. Or you can, through
living these statutes, find them at the heart of everything
that makes life livable.

Notice the grand contrast in the section that we have been
examining. The Lord says: "I will gather . . . I will assemble
. . . I will give." In every human situation we are given
material with which to work. We do not create it. But we
are responsible for the way we use it. So next God pictures
the human response of the returning exiles: "They will
remove . . . detestable things." But God is not done with
His people. "I will . . . give them a heart of flesh." And the
people are not done with responsibility. "That they may walk
in my statutes."

And now the conclusion, which is the controlling thought in the entire prophecy of Ezekiel. "They shall be my people, and I will be their God." This is a restatement of God's promise to Abraham. The double promise is found many other times in the Old Testament. This is its first occurrence in the gloomy *Book of Ezekiel,* which, you remember, is divided geometrically into two parts: the first, destruction, the second, rebuilding. Here in Chapter 11, close to the midpoint in the prophecy of destruction, we can almost hear the groans of the wounded while our eyes smart with smoke from burning homes. And here, where we most need it, is the promise, "They shall be my people, and I will be their God."

God is working out His purpose. This is, I believe, above all else the message we in the twentieth century need from Ezekiel. It is the intellectual fashion today to say that we live in a world of chance. We Christians believe that out of the primordial chaos God is bringing order. Contemporary thinkers have rediscovered chaos, which is at least a faint ground for hope that they may rediscover God, working within the shadows, and keeping watch upon His own. And we who are trying to live our faith amid the struggle find that in daily experience God is our refuge and our fortress, or, as Ezekiel calls Him our "little sanctuary."

Ezekiel 13:2-23

Son of man, prophesy against the prophets of Israel...who prophesy out of their own minds: "Hear the word of the Lord!"...

Woe to the foolish prophets who follow their own spirit, and have seen nothing! Your prophets have been like foxes among ruins, O Israel. You have not gone up into the breaches, or built up a wall for the house of Israel, that it might stand in battle in the day of the Lord. They have spoken falsehood and divined a lie; they say, "Says the Lord," when the Lord has not sent them, and yet they expect him to fulfill their word....

Because you have uttered delusions and seen lies...behold, I am against you....My hand will be against the prophets who see delusive visions and who give lying divinations; they shall not be in the council of my people, nor be enrolled in the register of the house of Israel, nor shall they enter the land of Israel; and you shall know that I am the Lord God....

Because they have misled my people, saying, "Peace," when there is no peace; and because, when the people build a wall, these prophets daub it with whitewash; say to those who daub it with whitewash that it shall fall! There will be a deluge of rain, great hailstones will fall; and a stormy wind break out; and when the wall falls will it not be said to you, "Where is the daubing with which you daubed it?"...

I will make a stormy wind break out in my wrath; and there shall be a deluge of rain in my anger, and great hailstones in wrath to destroy it. And I will break down the wall that you have daubed with whitewash ,and bring it down to the ground, so that its foundation will be laid bare; when it falls, you shall perish in the midst of it; and you shall know that I am the Lord....

And you, son of man, set your face against the daughters of your people, who prophesy out of their own minds; prophesy against them and say, "Thus says the Lord God: Woe to the women who sew magic bands upon all wrists, and make veils for the heads of persons of every stature, in the hunt for souls! Will you hunt down souls belonging to my people, and keep other souls alive for your profit? You have profaned me among my people for handfuls of barley and for pieces of bread, putting to death persons who should not die and keeping alive persons who should not live, by your lies to my people, who listen to lies....

"Because you have disheartened the righteous falsely, although I have not disheartened him, and you have encouraged the wicked, that he should not turn from his wicked way to save his life; therefore you shall no more see delusive visions nor practice divination; I will deliver my people out of your hand. Then you will know that I am the Lord."

PROPHETS THEN AND NOW
Ezekiel 13:2-23

Before Ezekiel's time, and after, three kinds of religious leaders guided Israel's spiritual life. Priests conducted the sacrificial acts and led the people in organized worship. Elders did what we call personal counseling, as they helped their friends in applying faith to specific cases. And the prophets — strange, lonely, misunderstood men, who were greatly revered after their earthly lives — spoke directly for God.

In the thirteenth chapter of his book, Ezekiel examines the prophet's task, negatively, by looking at those who did it wrong. Between his day and ours are so many differences that it may seem futile to explore the minister's work with Ezekiel guiding us. But underlying the differences are the resemblances. Prophets, true and false, dealt with people, just as ministers do. Prophets had about the same kinds of temptations that clergymen do today, and people twenty-five centuries ago had about the same kind of spiritual needs that still exist. Ezekiel's acerb criticism has often helped me to examine the work I am doing. It may help others to think about the same important, but almost always baffling, work of the ministry.

THE MINISTRY TODAY

Once, almost every minister was pastor of a congregation. Today a minister may be piloting an airplane over the Bolivian jungles, or taking a doctorate in African languages at the University of Paris so that he can translate the New Testament into an obscure tongue. He may be a chaplain with the armed forces or in some large institution. He may direct a television studio or edit a magazine. He may work at a neighborhood house in the slums, or in the luxurious high-rise apartments nearby. He may toil in the factories, or he may drive endless miles from lonely ranch-house to lonely ranch-house. Or he may be one of our much-criticized Church executives.

The old pattern, where the Church stood physically at the center of the worshiping community, is broken. I do not say that this rupture is bad or good. It is the situation that exists today. The place where a person sleeps may have little or no relevance to the actual center of the person's life. And the Church is trying, imperfectly as always, to reach people where they are, by whatever means will be effective. The question before us is not the technique of reaching people, where Ezekiel has little to tell us, but our relationship with the people we are trying to reach, and with God.

Since most of us are more familiar with the pastor's work in a local congregation than with any other form of ministry, we can take a quick look at all the ministry by examining the pastorate. The first thing we see is a fantastic amount of work. If the world could be saved by committee meetings, it would have been saved long ago. The pastor today superintends an organization, which, in his better moments, he calls the Body of Christ. Sometimes the members, and the pastor, forget. Sometimes feelings are ruffled, and always bills are coming due. It is possible to become completely absorbed in the mechanics of Church organization and administration. But this is not the end of the pastor's work, it is just maneuvering into position to begin it.

The pastor appears occasionally in public, preaching, teaching, speaking. If his public appearance is to be worthwhile, he must spend long hours in private, getting ready. The congregation is least likely to understand this part of the minister's work. If I am invited to a meeting that I cannot attend because of a wedding rehearsal, I find complete, sympathetic understanding. But if I say that I must stay home to read a book, a brow furrows and the impression comes across that somehow I am neglecting my duty for frivolous enjoyment.

A pastor spends long hours counseling with troubled people in sickness and sorrow, or discussing questions about marriage, family, employment, habits that need to be developed or perhaps broken. Whatever happens to people is grist for the pastor's mill. And, somehow, with ten thousand claims upon his time, a pastor is supposed to take care of his own spiritual life. Once I had a long talk with a badly discouraged young minister, to whom I said, "You preach excellent sermons about prayer for other people. Listen to yourself for a change, and do what you've been talking about."

Ministers sometimes envy their friends in other lines of work. The manager of a shoe store, for example, knows that he is doing a good job if sales this year are a comfortable percentage above sales for last year. And, may the good Lord forgive us, many people judge the pastor's work by the same criteria they would use for a business man. If the membership is increasing and the budget is written in large figures with black ink, many beam and say, "What a wonderful pastor."

A thoughtful friend is a Church executive who works with city churches throughout the nation. He said, "One of the hardest tasks I have is trying to encourage good, strong men in dwindling communities. The character of the neighborhood has changed. The Apostle Paul himself couldn't produce any impressive statistics. And the poor man works his heart out and blames himself because the church isn't growing." The executive thought about this for a moment, then he added, "There's one kind of minister who's worse, though. And that's the fellow in a rapidly expanding suburb, where it's almost impossible to keep the church from growing, and he takes all the credit for himself." My friend thought a while longer, and said, "You people in Florida are the worst about this." Then, after a long pause, he added, "But they're pretty bad in California, too."

On those rare occasions when the normal frictions of congregational life have quieted down to a dull roar, when the budget is balanced for the time being, and Sunday

School attendance is increasing, I recall our Savior's words, "Woe to you when all men speak well of you." However, I know a small number of ministers who take the admonition so deeply to heart that they seem anxious to affront kind, decent Christians. They call it shocking people into awareness. Others call it bad manners. It has the result that all do not speak well of them, but I don't think this is what the Lord intended.

An effort to make necessary change, in the Church or anywhere else, will produce friction. A clergyman worth his salt is prepared to accept the result of doing what is necessary. He has Ezekiel's warning in mind: "Though briers and thorns are with you and you sit upon scorpions; be not afraid." But some clergy seem to run around looking for scorpions to sit on, which is simply the Protestant version of the hair-shirt.

Staying out of trouble is no guarantee that a clergyman is a success, but neither is getting into trouble. Impressive earthly statistics may bear little or no relation to the statistics written in the Lamb's Book of Life. Some highly paid clergy are spiritually bankrupt, some on miserable incomes are spiritually rich, and some, likewise on miserable incomes, are grossly overpaid. How are you going to judge success or failure in a kind of work where the criteria are invisible and intangible? Perhaps Ezekiel can help us, with his scorching blast at the false prophets.

PROPHETS, FALSE

The Hebrew word translated prophet means "he who speaks." The English word comes from the Greek language, where *pro* means both "fore" and "forth," and *phetes* means "teller" or "speaker." So a prophet is one who forth-tells, or occasionally fore-tells. The Old Testament uses the term quite loosely, including strong men like Ezekiel and Jeremiah and spiritual weaklings like Baalam. Young Saul encountered a band of prophets, similar to the modern dervishes who express their faith in vigorous physical activity. Amos said, "I am no prophet nor a prophet's son." Today we think of Amos as *the* prophet of his day. We have forgotten the professional ecstatics whose company he would not claim. The fact that a person calls himself a prophet, or a clergyman, is no guarantee that he speaks for God.

The New Testament has a convenient term, "false prophet," which we can apply to some people who lived and worked in Babylon during Ezekiel's time. A stormy passage in Jeremiah names three: Ahab, Zedekiah, and Shemiah. Jeremiah adds one detail that Ezekiel, strangely, overlooks. (Ezekiel seldom overlooked anything scandalous.) The Jerusalem prophet says that two of these three men, in addition to prophesying falsely, denied the faith by their sexual conduct. Strong, godly men have slipped. God has forgiven them and the Church has forgiven them. Even so, conduct away from the pulpit remains an important test of a clergyman's work.

Ezekiel lumps his criticism into one thought: God's false representatives "prophesy out of their own minds." A person who speaks in public about spiritual matters is given, willy-nilly, the present world situation with which he and his hearers must deal. Within this context he must choose what to preach. He can, if so inclined, give good advice, or he can proclaim the mind of the Lord. If he is a person of wide experience and deep thought, the advice may be very good, but a young man, like Ezekiel, should be quite hesitant about offering his own opinion to his elders.

Centuries later another saint gave a young friend some apparently contradictory instructions. He said: "Be urgent in season and out of season, convince, rebuke, and exhort." And he said likewise: "Let no one despise your youth." A young man who throws his weight around, delivering profundities and rebukes from the depth of his inexperience, tempts all right thinking people to despise his youth. The Apostle urges that young Timothy be tactful in his rebuking, but tact by itself does not resolve the minister's dilemma: that a weakling must help other weaklings to be strong. The Apostle states positively what Ezekiel states negatively: "Preach the Word." The person who represents God — be he minister, prophet, Sunday School teacher, or whatnot — boldly and forcibly proclaims the Word; for it is not his own mind he offers, but God's. He honestly labels his own opinions as such. When he speaks with authority, it is God's authority.

In his autobiography Dr. Martin Niemöller, the German submarine commander who became a clergyman, and whose staunch loyalty to Jesus Christ brought inevitable conflict with Adolf Hitler, tells about his first sermon while a student in theological seminary. He describes the worry with which most seminary students are only too familiar. He delivered the sermon before the class, and believed that he had failed; so he sought an opportunity to preach to a congregation, where as he spoke he actually heard the sacred words that his lips were uttering, "My soul doth magnify the Lord." He tells that ever since his only preaching worry has been whether or not the message genuinely comes from God.

I cannot claim to have achieved victory over worry, as a preacher or in any other capacity. But often enough, when I feel impelled to say something that will arouse opposition, I apply Dr. Niemöller's test. Is this the contemporary expression of God's Word? Or is this my idea about what the Lord would have said if He had thought of it? If the former, I say it. If the latter, the good Lord usually gives me enough sense to keep quiet.

A prophet represented God; a false prophet represented his own opinion as God's. Some of Ezekiel's thoughts are difficult to understand and difficult to translate into twentieth-century language, but not this one. The understanding and the translation are easy. It's the application to my own work that hurts.

And now we look for an unsavory moment at the hags who vended witchcraft in the name of God, and called it prophecy. The Old Testament mentions, with profound respect, honorable, godly prophetesses. They served the Lord faithfully in their several communities, and today are serving Him in eternity. Ezekiel is not picturing such, but those who sold good luck, which is always a more popular commodity than righteousness.

In the city where I live professional fortune-tellers are not permitted to hawk their wares, but the county is a bit more lenient, and so, just beyond the city borders are fascinating signs, advertising that Madame Bushwah will read your

palm for a dollar, or Señora Decepción will gaze into a
crystal ball on your behalf for the same price. The local
Voodoo merchants do not advertise, but if you really wish to
put a hex on someone (we call it a conjur in these parts) it
can be arranged. A small doll, with a suitable set of impre-
cations muttered over it, is pierced with several pins, where-
upon your enemy is supposed to develop pains in the appro-
priate spot. Pitiful? Yes. Horrible? Yes. Disgusting? Yes.
Profitable? Evidently.

Men and women who in other ways appear quite sensible
turn to witchcraft for guidance through matters where common sense would tell them to consult an attorney, an invest-
ment counsellor, a physician, or a pastor. The ultimate
tragedy is that some people vend sorcery in the name of
Jesus Christ, who came to liberate us from superstition,
among other things. It was much the same in Ezekiel's day.
Even the techniques of witchcraft are almost unchanged.

The Son of Man asks the fortune-tellers: "Will you hunt
down souls belonging to my people, and keep other souls
alive for your profit?"

There we were, comfortably talking about someone else,
over whom I can easily feel contemptuous superiority, and
all of a sudden Ezekiel has hit me between the eyes again.

I am a minister. I draw a salary. Further, ever since I have
been actively engaged in Church work, I have been doing
everything I can do to raise the lowest salaries paid within
our denomination. The low-salaried men demonstrate a
keen interest in the matter. But likewise, the warm heart of
the Church responds, when people know the existing need.
(I have also proposed that the Church put a maximum
limit upon salaries. This engenders an equally keen but not
quite so sympathetic response from the high-salaried men.)

What is the reason for all the hustle and bustle that make
up Church life? The pay check? Or the human beings whom
Jesus Christ came to save? People have material needs.
Clergymen are people. Therefore clergymen have material
needs. The offering is an important part of morning worship.
I bless the offering, asking the Heavenly Father to use it for
the Savior's glory, and then a good-sized chunk of it comes
to me as a pay-check.

I try to realize, when I am buying a pair of shoes, that the purchase price is dedicated money, given to carry on the work of Christ in the community. I keep hoping that the money I receive is a necessary means for me to continue doing Christ's work, and that it will always remain far down the list of important considerations. If I am serving God to make money, then in all decency I ought to go into some kind of work where money-making is aboveboard and honest. I keep hoping that I accept money — consecrated money — only in order that I may continue trying to serve the Lord.

In a brief poem, *How to Become a Hypocrite,* the Scottish Christian poet, Ian Cowie, has well expressed some questions that ought occasionally to prod a minister's conscience.

> Have I used eternal truths as if they were just my stock-in-trade?
> Have I made the Gospel of Christ a mere means to bolster my own reputation?
> Have I prostituted goodness by making it pay?
>   . . . . . .
> When my light shines before men, whom does it glorify? me—or my Father in Heaven?
>   . . . . . .
> Save me, O Christ, from hypocrisy, I cannot save myself.
>   . . . . . .
> Lord have mercy upon me, Christ have mercy upon me.

THE WALL

Ezekiel illustrates by picturing a city wall that God's self-appointed representatives — male and female — have failed. Jerusalem was a city set on a hill, surrounded by a massive stone wall for protection against enemy attack. When the exiles returned to their homeland, a generation after Ezekiel's message, they began almost at once to rebuild the wall, and they found it necessary to station armed guards to protect the builders. Nehemiah tells in fascinating detail how the work was organized; how the High Priest, the goldsmith, the perfumer, the merchant, and the civil magistrate took responsibility for various parts of the wall, while their brothers stood by with sword and spear. Every citizen's duty was to build and defend the wall.

Ezekiel's wall is figurative for Israel's defenses — spiritual, political, economic. In the critical hour the false prophets neither helped to build a firm defense nor did they stand guard. The prophet uses an unusual word to suggest a wall built of stone but chinked together with mud or untempered mortar.

A wall that is carefully built will endure for centuries. The master craftsmen in ancient Peru, for instance, cut stone with incredible precision and laid it in place for the ages. Barring earthquake or other natural catastrophe, their walls will stand for millenia to come. A poorly built wall — as many a fireman's widow can testify — will collapse when subject to unusual strain, endangering the life of any who entrusts himself to its strength.

Strains come upon walls, both the kind built from stones and the kind Ezekiel is talking about, a people's spiritual, political, and economic defenses. He has said that the institutions in Israel are shabbily constructed, comparable to a flimsy wall which might look quite impressive but could not stand up against even a driving rainstorm.

It is every responsible citizen's duty to help build the wall or to defend it. His individual effort will not avail if the wall itself is rotten. A mason might cut and trim stones to perfection, but if others tumble his stone into place and daub it with poorly mixed mortar, the wall will be dangerous. Less figuratively, the account executive, the school teacher, the truck driver and the plumber are helping to build a decent society when they do their work well, if the framework within which they labor is sound. A school-teacher, for instance, who teaches children to accept a rotten social system is destroying rather than building, while one who works within a basically decent social system, and teaches children to evaluate its strength and its weakness, is among God's master-craftsmen in building the kind of world He desires for us.

The prophet has the same responsibilities that every other citizen knows, plus a few that are his because he is a prophet. He must examine the whole fabric of society — the wall — and point out its strength and its defects. The world needs responsible critics. We have enough professional viewers-with-alarm, whose incessant yakety-yak adds to our confusion, which is now and always has been considerable. The true spokesman for God helps the layman to be a saint (a New Testament word) who will make his unique contribution to building the wall, and he examines the wall itself for dangerous cracks.

The false prophets daubed the wall with whitewash. We still use Ezekiel's picturesque expression. Someone in government makes a grotesque error. After much investigation, a person in high places issues a report, crying, " 'Peace,' when there is no peace." (Patrick Henry knew a good line when he saw it.) We read the report and throw down the newspaper, muttering, "A splendid whitewash job."

We ought to understand what Ezekiel is talking about, whether or not we profit by it. In the United States today a weird alliance exists between liberal theology and liberal politics. Another alliance, equally weird, exists between conservative theology and conservative politics. You can tell, with about 80 per cent accuracy, what a Christian believes about the government's involvement in the electric industry by discovering his views on the inspiration of the Holy Scripture. One theologian daubs with whitewash anything labelled "liberal." God knows how much shabby legislation our country has suffered under this rubric. Another seems quite willing to baptize as the immutable will of God anything and everything dating from the days of Rutherford B. Hayes, not all of which is worth conserving. A prophet ought to stand beyond his own prejudices and desires. He ought to try to look at the world from the divine perspective. And when he has nothing to say, other than his own opinions, he ought in common decency not to blame them on the Almighty.

JUDGMENT

The entire first half of Ezekiel's prophecy is given over to judgment. Kings and priests are judged. Captains and merchants are judged. Farmers and their wives are judged. And prophets are judged. Judgment does not automatically mean the sentence of guilt. An earthly judge has the weighty responsibility of determining the fact before passing the sentence. The divine judge determines the fact: "You have uttered delusions and seen lies." He passes the sentence:

"Therefore behold I am against you." One man, with God, is a majority. The whole world, against God, is lost.

Everything in the Bible, after the third chapter, tells what God is doing to bring a lost world back to itself, which means back to God. Sometimes I think the most important thought in the whole Bible comes in the Parable of the Prodigal Son, "When he came to himself he said . . . 'I will arise and go to my Father.'" Christ came into the world to save people: prodigal sons, account-executives, school teachers, truck drivers, plumbers — and ministers. Such people are His agents in saving the world when they obey His will. Both Ezekiel and the New Testament teach that in the long run our divine Judge will triumph. The question before the individual is whether or not he wishes to contribute to the triumph. The judgment is God's decision about the matter.

It is fashionable today to think of judgment as the historical dynamic, where greed brings about its own destruction and tyranny begets rebellion. Certainly Ezekiel shows the vast panorama of change, with empires toppling and new forces emerging from the ruin. But also he shows us something quite different, which we are examining at the moment. History consists of many individual acts. We are here thinking about the actions and judgment of the individual who claims to represent the Heavenly Father in a world that is—in the only legitimate sense of the term—going to hell.

God's judgment against the individuals who misrepresent Him is stern: "My Hand will be against the prophets who see delusive visions." Ezekiel was guided by God's Hand. (The New Testament adopts Ezekiel's other expression for the same reality, God's Spirit, which means breath.) The Hand of God guides and restrains, and frequently gives an encouraging clap on the shoulder. The same Hand can smite with devastating power.

Ezekiel teaches that historical catastrophe is an expression of divine judgment, in the midst of which the man of faith is responsible to live his faith. Here he pictures a catastrophe —obviously the fall of Jerusalem—as a poorly built wall collapsing. A hurricane-force wind drives torrential rains against the wall. The whitewash melts instantly. The shoddy mortar begins to wash. The heavy stones, poorly cut and clumsily laid, shift, and their weight brings down the wall in hideous collapse. The people who thought themselves safe behind the wall ask their mentors, "Where is the daubing with which you daubed it?"

The outstanding modern example of Ezekiel's dour prophecy is Russia. The Church, under the tsars, included many godly members and leaders who spoke out strongly for social justice, sometimes at risk of their lives. But many more, in places of high leadership, applied whitewash with a wide brush, as the cracks in the wall grew wider and more dangerous. The wall fell, and the foolish prophets along with it.

Ezekiel will never let us stop when we have critically analyzed another person's failure. How about us, citizens of the United States, in the last third of the twentieth century. Obviously the wall our fathers built was sound. It has survived. But, as Robert Frost reminds us, "Something there is that does not love a wall." Even the gigantic stones at Machu Picchu may eventually be toppled by the slow growth of roots between the cracks.

Our American Way of Life—which we seem to be turning into a graven image—contains much good, but it is not all good. Not everything in modern society comes close to God's will. I suspect, for instance, that our agricultural policy, if any one could understand it, would be conclusive proof that man has fallen from grace. Many giant corporations are deservedly praised for their fairness with all their employees. Others have been forced by union pressure into relatively decent employment policies. But these latter corporations still employ the ethic of the jungle in dealing with middle-management. (I could illustrate the remark at length, and with heat.) Abuses of union power are known. And, as far as private morality is concerned, have you read *Peyton Place?* (I don't recommend it if you haven't.) This is the story of a picture-post-card village, neatly bracketed between two picture-post-card Churches, one Congregational and the other Roman Catholic, which the best people regard with varying degrees of contempt, and from which the other villagers stay away in droves, while illustrating by their lives that man without God is lost. Fiction? Yes, the names are fictitious. The failures and sorrows described are not.

In this crazy, mixed-up, lost world God has called some of us to be His ministers. Our times are no more confused than Jeremiah's and Ezekiel's. And I, for one, have found their analysis of prophecy in another age helpful to my ministry today. Jeremiah tells me that a minister's conduct away from the pulpit is not his private business. He serves— or denies—God with every act. Ezekiel has told us to keep an unremitting eye on our motives. It is easy to preach for pay, and easier to keep silent when an unpopular remark might diminish the offering. But the bulk of Ezekiel's wisdom to us comes in his scathing blast against those who "prophesy out of their own minds." It would be a welcome gust of cool air if the ministers in our time who do not know God's will would keep quiet.

We have a considerable volume of what we profess to be God's written message to us. Its meaning is not all on the surface. It does not answer many insistent questions. But it gives the answer to life's biggest question: What must I do to be saved? And it lays down some guidelines of honor, duty, justice, and charity that apply to individuals, corporations, and governments. If we are faithful to proclaim what we know, perhaps in time the Lord will enable us to see what we do not yet know. That is what Ezekiel's prophecy is all about: looking steadfastly to the flickering light in the midst of the storm cloud until the glory of God is visible.

The word of the Lord came to me again: "What do you mean by repeating this proverb...'The fathers have eaten sour grapes, and the children's teeth are set on edge'? As I live,...this proverb shall no more be used.... Behold, all souls are mine; the soul of the father as well as the soul of the son is mine: the soul that sins shall die.

"If a man is righteous and does what is lawful and right—if he does not eat upon the mountains or lift up his eyes to the idols of the house of Israel, does not defile his neighbor's wife,...does not oppress anyone, but restores to the debtor his pledge, commits no robbery, gives his bread to the hungry and covers the naked with a garment, does not lend at interest or take any increase, withholds his hand from iniquity, executes true justice between man and man, walks in my statutes, and is careful to observe my ordinances—he is righteous, he shall surely live....

"If he begets a son who is a robber, a shedder of blood, who does none of these duties, but eats upon the mountains, defiles his neighbor's wife, oppresses the poor and needy, commits robbery, does not restore the pledge, lifts up his eyes to the idols, commits abomination, lends at interest, and takes increase; shall he then live? He shall not live. He has done all these abominable things; he shall surely die....

"But if this man begets a son who sees all the sins which his father has done, and fears, and does not do likewise,...but gives his bread to the hungry and covers the naked with a garment, withholds his hand from iniquity, takes no interest or increase, observes my ordinances, and walks in my statutes; he shall not die for his father's iniquity; he shall surely live....

"Yet you say, 'Why? does not the son bear the iniquity of the father?'[1]

"When the son has done what is lawful and right,...he shall surely live. The soul that sins shall die. The son shall not suffer for the iniquity of the father, nor the father suffer for the iniquity of the son; the righteousness of the righteous shall be upon himself, and the wickedness of the wicked shall be upon himself.

"But if a wicked man turns away from all his sins which he has committed and keeps all my statutes and does what is lawful and right, he shall surely live; he shall not die. None of the transgressions which he has committed shall be remembered against him;

---

[1] Adapted from the Authorized Version.

for the righteousness which he has done he shall live. Have I any pleasure in the death of the wicked, ... and not rather that he should turn from his way and live? But when a righteous man turns away from his righteousness and commits iniquity and does the same abominable things that the wicked man does, shall he live? ... For the ... sin he has committed, he shall die. ...

"Yet the house of Israel says, 'The way of the Lord is not just.' O house of Israel, are my ways not just? Is it not your ways that are not just? ...

"I will judge you, O house of Israel, every one according to his ways. ... Repent and turn from all your transgressions. ... Cast away from you all the transgressions which you have committed against me, and get yourselves a new heart and a new spirit! Why will you die, O house of Israel? For I have no pleasure in the death of anyone, ... so turn, and live."

RESPONSIBILITY
Ezekiel 18:1-32

Most students believe that Ezekiel's major contribution to our faith is his heavy emphasis upon individual responsibility. A few silly people have said that by emphasizing individuality the prophet loses sight of the balancing truth: the responsible individual is a member of society. Rather than trying to refute this criticism, I ask you to read the prophecy for yourself, where Ezekiel reminds his hearers almost endlessly that they are inextricably members of a spiritual and political community, the house of Israel.

Contemporary thought in the United States is lopsided, as Ezekiel is not. Some emphasize our collective responsibilities, almost forgetting that society consists of individuals. Others emphasize the rugged individual so much that they seem to ignore his neighbors, with whose lives his own is bound by uncountable ties. Man is part of society. Society consists of individual men. Both statements are true. Both are important. In the eighteenth chapter of Ezekiel, we are thinking about the individual and his direct responsibility to God.

THE HAND OF THE PAST

The individual is not the master of his fate. He comes into a world filled with circumstance that he did not create. The hand of the past lies heavy upon him. Twice during my lifetime, for example, my country has become involved in a war between France and Germany, which began, essentially, in the dynastic squabbles among Louis, Lothair, and Charles the Bald, following the death of Charlemagne. With occasional interruptions of peace, the war has been going on for the past thousand years. The men of our time who have fought in this long continued war did not start it.

Another illustration. The major internal difficulty we encounter in the United States stems from the fact that the human race comes in different colors, and people of one hue frequently dislike or distrust people of another hue. I believe that we Americans (black or white) are not much worse than any other people in this regard, but we are, individually and collectively, responsible to improve a situation that began in 1518, when the first slave ship unloaded its unhappy cargo in the Americas.

Ezekiel's companions in exile, like us, were caught in a situation they did not create, where almighty God called them to make their lives count. They were shut away from their homeland because King Jehoiakim had been foolish. Religious thinkers among them traced the spiritual infection back to the wounds, still festering, inflicted upon Israel in the days of King Manasseh, whose activities you can read about in the second Book of Kings or Chronicles. While you are reading you will notice, I hope, that faith in God has survived some perilous days before now. Unhappily, the religious leaders told the exiles that they were being punished for Manasseh's sin. The insight was valid, but the way it was expressed would discourage any sensible person's faith.

Manasseh sinned, hideously. Almost a century later good people suffered. It did not console them deeply to be told that they were guilty of his sin. Unconsciously they knew what Ezekiel put into words: guilt and righteousness are personal. Abraham might well bequeath many blessings to his descendants; he could not make them individually righteous. King Manasseh could—and did—bequeath pain to his grandchildren, but not guilt.

When a person is caught in a historical crisis that he did not create, but where he is called to play the man, it is easy for him to become cynical. The Hebrew people, both in Jerusalem and in Babylon, had a bitter proverb, "The fathers have eaten sour grapes, and the children's teeth are set on edge." It is one thing—and a good thing—to deflect the slings and arrows of outrageous fortune with a wry jest.

Neither Ezekiel nor any other who loves his fellow man would begrudge a person in sorrow the comfort of joking about his troubles. But the exiles were doing something quite different. They were running away from responsibility, and covering their guilt with barbed jokes against God and His justice.

I have mentioned the racial troubles in the United States today. I believe that these troubles can be ended only by the incessant application of charity to particular situations. Legislation has a necessary, though minor, part, in racial justice. And for the past ten years I have heard, on the average of once a day, the cynical quip, "You can't legislate morality." No, in a sense, you can't. But most of those who make the quip are revealing an attitude toward their dark-skinned neighbors, rather than a shallow understanding of the balance between law and grace. It is far easier to make cynical wise-cracks than to practice Christian love.

You and I did not make the mess, or series of messes, we are in. The exiled Hebrews did not make the mess they were in. But you and I, like the exiles in former time, are called to play the man at a particular time in history. We are individually responsible to improve, if we can, the mess our fathers bequeathed us. Ezekiel says the first essential in correcting social evils is to correct all the wrong in your individual relationship with God.

GOD AND THE INDIVIDUAL

Each man is a part of society, yet each man stands alone. If a new-born child is not almost immediately taken up into his mother's care, he will die. And yet he who at birth is embraced by another is an individual, who differs from every other individual in the world. When he reaches the age of responsible choice, he must make moral decisions, and these are lonely things. Small wonder that people flee the burden of responsibility, and turn to an infallible Church or an infallible state rather than face the awful loneliness of moral decision. Finally each individual must die. Others may stand at his bedside, offering what consolation they can. Death remains an individual matter.

Ezekiel was ministering to exiles who would die, biologically. They wanted to die spiritually, or at least go to sleep. They were shirking their moral responsibility. They wanted to accept the neighborhood standards, and to drift with the tide. They felt that God had failed them. They did not want to be reminded that God calls each person to return untarnished to Him the gift of life. They felt that God was punishing them for their father's sins, and they wanted quietly to forget about God. To meet this situation, Ezekiel spoke what many believe the most important sentence in his prophecy, "Behold, all souls are mine; the soul of the father as well as the soul of the son is mine; the soul that sins shall die."

Ezekiel had the unfortunate habit of stating positive truth negatively, which is one major reason why this prophecy is so much neglected today. He could just as truly have said, "The soul that is righteous will live," and his words would be beloved wherever there are Christians.

Interpreters have gone miles out of their way to misunderstand Ezekiel, who talks about "life" and "death," and illustrates with case studies of persons who "live" or "die." Some interpreters actually have said that Ezekiel is promising that the person who is righteous will survive until the exiles return to Jerusalem, and others that he is promising a long life to the righteous and swift extinction to the wicked. Every person other than Ezekiel knows that God does not work in this manner. Surely we might give Ezekiel credit for being as observant as the rest of us. In all the rest of his prophecy he speaks symbolically. Why should the eighteenth chapter be a lorn exception?

Life can mean biological existence, or it can mean awareness of God. Death can mean the end of biological function, or it can mean alienation from God. Here Ezekiel is using the terms life and death in their profound, spiritual meaning. Neither here nor anywhere else does he uphold faith as the great good-luck charm. He has told us, and there is no reason to think he has changed his mind, that the path of faith may lead to a crown of thorns and a cross. He has told us also that the one who endures the crown of thorns with God has a blessedness—here called life—unknown to the neighbor who may be wallowing in godless good luck. So when Ezekiel speaks to you of "life" and "death," do not join the foolish people who read his words without understanding. He is talking about the essential relation of life, which may be strong and vigorous while physical life is ebbing, or weak when biological vitality is superb. The soul that is righteous shall live with God.

Each individual Hebrew belonged to the Chosen People, who had a divinely given mission that could be fulfilled only as individual Hebrews responded to God, while the fortunes of the Chosen People were rising or falling with the political and economic changes in the Middle East. In time of prosperity, a person is tempted to credit himself for the blessings he enjoys. In time of adversity, the individual is tempted to blame all his trouble upon his forebears, his enemies, or God. It is only right and proper that one should examine as carefully as possible the historical events that have led to a particular tragedy. Ezekiel helped his fellow-exiles to do just this. But in the midst of the tragedy, the individual still is responsible to God for his actions. By the banks of the Chebar, faith — or spiritual life — still is possible.

Nobody else can be righteous for you. You cannot be righteous for anybody else. One generation cannot give spiritual life to another. Neither can one generation steal spiritual life from another. No man can hide, spiritually, behind his family, his tribe, his nation. You are individually, personally responsible to God for the way you live in a world you did not create.

THE PRACTICE OF FAITH

The theme of individual responsibility runs all through Ezekiel's prophecy. Here in the eighteenth chapter it is presented in its sharpest focus. Ezekiel illustrates a principle with several case studies in faith. He knew, just as you and I know, that human conduct is more complex than the illustrations would indicate. Most bad people have some wonderfully good qualities, and most good people have some distressingly bad qualities. To illustrate a principle, a teacher of chemistry today sets up a laboratory demonstration, from which everything extraneous to the point at issue is excluded, and no one thinks the less of him for it. In exactly the same sense, Ezekiel illustrates what he is talking about. Without naming names, he refers to Abraham, the righteous father, and Manasseh, the evil son. The grandson is Ezekiel's contemporary neighbor, the exiled Hebrew.

Were you or I writing the illustration, we would choose different aspects of spiritual life, but we can profit by looking at those Ezekiel used. The righteous man does not "eat upon the mountains," or actively engage in pagan worship. More significant, he does not "lift up his eyes to the idols of the house of Israel." This was the gravest danger in Ezekiel's time, as in ours, not defiant departure from faith, but the slow admixture of alien elements into the faith. I forebear to illustrate from modern time.

Second, the righteous man holds marriage sacred. He respects the personality of his own wife, and that of his neighbor's wife. Again, I could illustrate from modern time, but will not.

Third, the righteous man practices his faith with his pocketbook. In business transactions, he recognizes that he is dealing with people, and that people are more important than profits. The central political and social struggles in the United States today swirl about this economic issue.

Fourth, and last, the righteous man "walks in my statutes, and is careful to observe my ordinances."

At the end of his prophecy, Ezekiel shows us a Temple, and a life-giving stream that flows from it. The stream accomplishes its miracles far away from the Temple, out where people earn and spend, and live and love. Our idea of piety as to what you do in Church or at private worship is badly askew. The Carpenter of Nazareth wants to be at your side while you are hammering nails, or whatever passes for hammering nails in your life.

A righteous life is possible even by the River Chebar, not easy, but possible. So is the opposite. The righteous man described has a son who denies by his life all that the father has affirmed. Each generation gives much that is good—along with much that is not so good—to the next. But one generation cannot pass righteousness to another. The evil man "shall surely die." He may live in a palace, where a host of flunkies carry out his slightest bidding, but spiritually he is dead.

"If this man begets a son who sees all the sins which his father has done, and fears... he shall surely live." The Hebrews have a tradition that the reader does not pronounce the word "fears," but instead he says, "a son who sees all the sins which his father has done and *considers*... he shall surely live." The tradition expresses exactly what Ezekiel is driving at. He is not giving a sterile analysis of moral life, he is calling for a decision. He is asking his contemporaries —and you—to consider, to repent, to live. The sins of the past cannot deprive you of spiritual life, unless you wish to be deprived.

Ezekiel is the lonely herald of the individual in the days of the organization man. In our time of massive organization, the individual sometimes wonders if his life matters much one way or the other. It does. A left-fielder is indubitably a member of the baseball team. Yet, when the ball is coming his way and the sun is in his eyes, his performance as an individual is what counts. More significant, following a critical operation, a patient died of infection. After exhaustive inquiry, the Chief of Surgery discovered that the nurse who was responsible to sterilize the instruments had a date one evening, and so she left them in the autoclave less than the required time. She was a member of a team, but through her individual failure, a fellow man lost his physical life. Still more significant, a friend of mine, a pleasant-spoken, cultured gentleman, smiles quietly, and says, "My wife takes care of the religion for my family." He is destroying his spiritual life, and endangering that of his children, in a gracious and charming manner. He has not become a libertine. His business ethics are up to the community standard. But he is not relating his daily actions to Almighty God. Spiritually, he is dying on his feet.

Ezekiel addressed a group of people, most of them pleasant and charming, who were content to die on their feet. They did not wish to go to the intellectual effort of denying God. Neither did they wish to accept the responsibility of serving Him.

THE CALL TO LIFE

When you studied geometry all your proofs rested upon a few things taken for granted: axioms. Ezekiel states an axiom of faith. This is not something to be proved, it is something that every man of faith knows and accepts. "If a wicked man turns away from all his sins ... and does what is lawful and right, he shall surely live." This is repentance. Feeling sorry for the wrong you have done is remorse, if it goes no farther than just feeling sorry. Repentance means feeling sorry for the wrong you have done—not because you have been caught—and turning away from the wrong to live the right.

The exiles saw no need to repent, and no benefit if they did, since they were being punished for sins that someone else had committed. If they told God they were sorry for their individual sins—small acts of dishonesty and that sort of thing—what earthly difference would it make? They would still be exiled by an unfeeling tyranny, while their unworthy brothers back in Jerusalem were sneering at them.

From a completely different standing point, many today have reached exactly the same conclusions. "Repent? Me? Of what? We all make mistakes, and I've made a few myself. Besides, there are too many hypocrites in Church." The blithe assumption that one can be good without God is related to the fact that man has been incredibly successful in controlling many things; so he believes, unconsciously, that a little more of the same kind of effort that has eliminated smallpox will eliminate divorce.

Modern man has demonstrated an amazing ability to control things. I visited a factory recently, in which complex products are delivered, neatly boxed, at the end of a production line where no workers stand. At various stages in the process, strange tools shape the metal, drill and tap holes, and install parts that fit to minute tolerance. When a tool grows dull, it is automatically replaced by another. The requirements of the complex machine are telegraphed to the various stock-rooms. Several times a year comes a malfunction too great for the machine to correct, then it flashes a signal light and shuts down automatically, and people get to work. Obviously it required the finest kind of disciplined brainpower to produce such a machine. And, we all know, the greatest fear in the heart of the American working man is that he will be automated out of a job.

The fear of automation is not confined to workers on the production line. Once a corporation treasurer was guiding me through another great factory. I asked him if his duties normally include ushering visitors about the plant, and he said, "Not today. But looking down the road about five years, I can see my job being taken over by a little black box. And I'm getting into the public relations end of things before the rush starts."

Modern man has demonstrated his ability to control things. Today's technology overshadows that of any previous age. But somehow, when it comes to the human spirit, the same modern man shows an incredible ability to fall flat on his face. His very accomplishments create in their turn a host of spiritual disasters. Automation can produce things, but in the process it can destroy people. Each time I mention in public the sad results of automation, someone points to the telephone company, where automation has greatly increased the number of jobs available. I recognize the possible long-term benefits. But I wish that my friends would explain them to the unemployed coal-miners in eastern Kentucky. They are the ones who need convincing.

We have been operating for the past century or so on the genial assumption that if everyone just tries hard enough to make money, somehow things will turn out all right. Christian faith is in favor of money (or some viable means of exchange) and Christians are all in favor of people making money (or whatever will enable them to live in dignity.) But when our modern man asks innocently, "What is there for me to repent of?" we might mention that he has violated the first commandment by giving first place in life to a false deity that, among other things, is subject to inflation.

What's to do? Reform the economic system? I agree that changes should take place, as undoubtedly they will. But I do not join those Christians who find evil inherent in the private ownership and management of property. Our generation has witnessed reform of economic systems on a scale unprecedented in history. The result has not been particularly inspiring. As I write, an outstanding symbol of the reformed economic system is the Berlin Wall, which was designed to keep workers at their lathes and plows in East Germany, when they want to escape to the unreformed economic system of West Germany. (They have even stronger non-economic reasons for wishing to escape.)

Ezekiel foresaw changes greater than anything we can remotely contemplate. He foresaw an overthrow of the Babylonian Empire, which would enable the exiles to return to their home land. And he asked the individual Hebrew, as his share in the future, to straighten out his personal relationship with the Almighty. He did not think faith a private luxury, but he saw that underlying any political or social reform must come first the relationship between an individual and God, who asks, "Have I any pleasure in the death of the wicked ... and not rather that he should turn from his way and live?" Once more Ezekiel has said, negatively, what the world today is dying to hear positively stated.

God cares about you. God made you so that your life can respond to His love. God placed you in a particular historical setting, which He does not ask you to like. Rather, He asks that, whatever your standing place, you turn from there toward God. And, wherever you are, in whatever valley of the shadow, the Lord tells you, through Ezekiel, you can make your life count. This is what God wants. This is why God made you; so that you can find yourself in Him. You, an individual, count in the cosmic sweep of things. In this vast, impersonal, automated world, it matters what kind of person you are, because the Maker of heaven and earth cares about you. He cares so much that He made you His agent to make this His world.

In all reverence, we can call the events in which Ezekiel participated a dress rehearsal for God's final triumph on earth. The people through whom God chose to triumph had no individual social or political importance. They were exiles. And God promised to return them to their home, as a symbol that finally the human race will return to our true dwelling place. Before the scattered exiles could return, they must become spiritually fit to return. They must be alive. So must we.

The other Son of Man gives some practical guidance about the way of achieving life. He does not talk about necessary and important things, such as economic reform, He goes to the heart of reality, which is personal, and He says, "I am the Way, and the Truth, and the Life." Accept the truth embodied in Christ. Follow the path that He walks. And you will live.

Ezekiel 28:2-19

Son of man, say to the prince of Tyre, "Thus says the Lord God:
  'Because your heart is proud,
    and you have said, "I am a god,
  I sit in the seat of the gods,
    in the heart of the seas,"
  yet you are but a man, and no god,
    though you consider yourself as wise as a god—
  you are indeed wiser than Daniel;
    no secret is hidden from you;
  by your wisdom and your understanding
    you have gotten wealth for yourself,
  and have gathered gold and silver
    into your treasuries;
  by your great wisdom in trade
    you have increased your wealth,
    and your heart has become proud in your wealth—...

  'Because you consider yourself
    as wise as a god,
  therefore, behold, I will bring strangers upon you,
    the most terrible of the nations;
  and they shall draw their swords against
    the beauty of your wisdom
    and defile your splendor.
  They shall thrust you down into the Pit,
    and you shall die the death of the slain
    in the heart of the seas.
  Will you still say, "I am a god,"
    in the presence of those who slay you,
  though you are but a man, and no god,
    in the hands of those who wound you?...

'You were the signet of perfection,
    full of wisdom
    and perfect in beauty.
You were in Eden, the garden of God;
    every precious stone was your covering,
carnelian, topaz, and jasper,
    chrysolite, beryl, and onyx,
sapphire, carbuncle, and emerald;
    and wrought in gold were your settings
    and your engravings.
On the day that you were created
    they were prepared.
With an anointed guardian cherub I placed you;
    you were on the holy mountain of God;
    in the midst of the stones of fire you walked.
You were blameless in your ways
    from the day you were created,
    till iniquity was found in you.

'In the abundance of your trade,
    you were filled with violence, and you sinned;
So I cast you as a profane thing from the mountain of God,
    and the guardian cherub drove you out
    from the midst of the stones of fire.
Your heart was proud because of your beauty;
    you corrupted your wisdom for the sake of your splendor.
I cast you to the ground;
    I exposed you before kings,
    to feast their eyes on you.
By the multitude of your iniquities,
    in the unrighteousness of your trade
    you profaned your sanctuaries;
so I brought forth fire from the midst of you;
    it consumed you,
and I turned you to ashes upon the earth
    in the sight of all who saw you.
All who know you among the peoples
    are appalled at you;
you have come to a dreadful end
    and shall be no more for ever.' "

A CRITICAL LOOK AT A
COMMERCIAL CIVILIZATION
Ezekiel 28:2-19

Jerusalem has fallen. The prophet's tragic warning is fulfilled. Now Ezekiel must persuade the despairing exiles that God, who apparently has lost a battle, will win the war. The symbol of divine victory is the return to Jerusalem, for which Ezekiel teaches his people to hope and live and work. He gets to his task in a leisurely and roundabout way, by examining seven hostile nations. Seven, of course, is the symbol for completeness, telling that God is Lord over the entire earth. Two of the seven nations concern us in particular: Egypt symbolizes military power, and Tyre commercial power. We have necessarily thought much about military force when reading Ezekiel. Now we look through the prophet's eyes at a commercial civilization. Do I need to remind you that we are a commercial civilization? If you treat the section about Tyre as an exercise in ancient history, you will find it filled with interest. If it helps you to examine your own motives in business life, you will find it the word of God to you.

THE PRINCE OF TYRE

Tyre was the capital city of the Phoenician civilization, lying in the shadow of the Lebanon Mountains, at the eastern end of the Mediterranean Sea. The city was built on a rocky island, about half a mile from the shore. Between the island and the mainland was a deep harbor. Behind Tyre lay the mountains, with their rich supply of ship-building timber. Before Tyre lay the world.

The Phoenicians took advantage of their opportunities. They built ships, the best afloat. They manned their ships with skillful sailors. Their daring explorers discovered the unknown. Just a few years before Ezekiel's time, the Egyptian Pharaoh sent a Phoenician exploring party on a voyage of discovery that ended by their circumnavigating Africa.

You remember that Solomon asked King Hiram of Tyre to provide structural timber, architects, and construction foremen for the Holy Temple. Among these foremen was a foundry-master who, like the King, was named Hiram. With all the metallurgical advances of three thousand years to help us, our best foundrymen today would have difficulty reproducing the work that Hiram did for the Temple. Solomon wanted the best, and nothing was better than Tyrian craftsmanship.

The peculiar genius of Tyre was not so much in sailing and building, where many other cultures have excelled, but in commerce. The Phoenicians purchased raw material from mine, farm, forest and sea, and made it usable. They transported the world's goods from place of origin to the place of need or want. As incidents to the process, they developed double-entry bookkeeping and the alphabet. The Egyptians and Babylonians had known forms of picture-writing. The Phoenicians assigned particular sounds, rather than meanings, to certain pictures. For example, the first letter of their alphabet was an ox, whose name was "aleph." The second letter was a house, named "beth."

A distinguished lecturer once addressed a women's club, telling the members something about the Phoenicians. When he had finished the chairman said, "I don't know how we ever can thank you." The lecturer rose, bowed, and said, "I forgot to mention that the Phoenicians likewise invented money."

In Ezekiel's day Ithobaal II ruled over Tyre. The twenty-eighth chapter of the prophecy concerns the Prince of Tyre, but not as an individual man; he stands instead as a symbol for the Phoenician culture, its strength and its weakness.

Surely what I have said indicates the kind of strength that faith must admire. Praise is scant in Ezekiel, yet when describing the Prince of Tyre, the gloomy prophet is lyrical. He understands that the business man, indeed the entire economic system, is an important factor in spiritual life. The qualities that make for business success are good. Only their abuse is evil. The Phoenicians showed resource, daring, imagination. They took gifts from God and used them with intelligence, which is one of the Lord's best gifts to us. Doing so, they made it possible for God's children in many lands to receive the good things He has created. The manufacturer and the merchant are God's agents, who form an essential part in the divine plan of salvation. Their work is just as holy as that of the pastor. Their work, like the pastor's, carries with it many grave spiritual dangers. As we examine the dangers, we must never forget that they are inherent in a good, necessary, and holy task.

A man who expects to stay in business must make a profit. (If government takes over the business, the identical somber truth remains, shrouded behind a subsidy.) Dollars are just as much a part of faith as hymnbooks. But it is easy to turn from serving God on the job and to serve a false deity, profit. Our Savior was a Builder, who came to help us build ships, houses, corporations, governments, and, most important, lives. Earning a profit can be an important part of spiritual life, constructively or destructively.

THE PRICE OF SUCCESS

Those who envy successful people frequently ignore one minor essential: Success is hard work. The president of a corporation puts in hours that he would never dare ask from his file clerk. But hard work by itself is not enough. Knowledge must be added to industry. What are the resources? What is possible? What are the obstacles? Even knowledge and energy are not enough. The subtle element of judgment must guide them. What things are worth doing? What things should be done first?

The combination of hard work, knowledge, and judgment is wrapped up in the old-fashioned word "gumption," which my grandmother used, mostly in reference to my lack of it. The Holy Bible, speaking about this quality of gumption, calls it wisdom. It is not the mere accumulation of knowledge, nor is it the mere exertion of effort, nor is it the skill of the grand-stand quarterback, who exercises perfect judgment without responsibility. Knowing what to do, and when to do it, and then doing it—this is wisdom. In this sense the Prince of Tyre was wise. He paid the price of success. He was successful.

THE DANGER OF SUCCESS

Nowhere in the entire Bible is the danger of success more clearly stated than in the poem we are considering. The Prince says, "I am a god, I sit in the seat of the gods." Some scholars argue that the Tyrians believed in the divinity of the king. This belief has troubled the world often enough, but it is not what Ezekiel is driving at. The beliefs of ancient Tyre really don't concern us much, it's you the Bible is talking about, not Ithobaal II. The Prince of Tyre has edged God from the throne, and has climbed upon the throne himself. This restates the message in Genesis where a couple of people said, in the first recorded manifestation of human pride, "If we just defy God in this small matter, we shall be as gods."

When people are picking and choosing which of the Ten Commandments they will consider important, inevitably they put the first commandment last. The Holy Spirit, working through Moses, put it first. "Thou shalt have no other gods before me." The Prince of Tyre chose to worship what William James called, "the bitch-goddess, Success." He was successful—or was he?

> By your wisdom and your understanding
>   you have gotten wealth for yourself,
> and have gathered gold and silver
>   into your treasuries;
> by your great wisdom in trade,
>   you have increased your wealth
>   and your heart has become proud in your wealth.

Wisdom is good. Success is good. Wealth is good. Pride is evil. That's the danger. The essence of pride is putting self into the place of God. This sin comes easily to successful people.

Theologians have struggled mightily to reconcile what Ezekiel says about the Prince of Tyre in the Garden of Eden with the accounts at the beginning of the Bible. If you look at the pictures, you will find all sorts of contradiction. If you look at the thing pictured, there is none. Genesis describes man in rebellion against God. Ezekiel describes one type of man, the successful business man, with the peculiar temptations that come to him because of his success.

> Every precious stone was your covering,
>   carnelian, topaz, and jasper...
> in the midst of the stones of fire you walked.

A man must be successful before he can purchase jewels. Ezekiel shows a man so successful that he tramples on gemstones.

Theologians have likewise troubled themselves overmuch about the doctrine of original sin and Ezekiel's glowing picture:

> You were blameless in your ways
>   from the day you were created,
>   till iniquity was found in you.

There is no contradiction. The Lord beheld the world He had made, and it was good. He beheld the human race whom He started on the perilous course to eternal life, and declared His workmanship good. The things with which the business man deals—he calls them raw materials—are good. The various acts of manufacturing and distributing useful products to people are good. Only the abuse of good is evil. This is the message in Genesis: that pride leads to irresponsible action, which leads to disaster. This is the message in Ezekiel.

When Adam and Eve sinned against God, they were cast from the Garden; so it was with the Prince of Tyre.

> In the abundance of your trade
>   you were filled with violence, and you sinned;
>   so I cast you as a profane thing from the mountain of
>   God....
> Your heart was proud because of your beauty;
>   you corrupted your wisdom for the sake of your splendor.

Has any pen ever written a more profound analysis of what is wrong with our civilization? "You corrupted your wisdom for the sake of your splendor."

The Phoenician civilization shows wisdom at work. Look at our civilization. Think about the complex of highways and airlines and railways joining farms and mines and factories to the distributors who deliver necessities to people. This results from wisdom, discipline, and skill of the highest order. Are these dedicated to the service of God? or "corrupted" to serve "splendor"?

THE GOAL OF OUR STRIVING

I receive through the mail about equal amounts of printed material, asking me as a clergyman either to help overthrow our present economic system or to uphold and defend it. Some of the latter makes it sound as if the most important work of Jesus Christ on earth is to insure the continuation of free enterprise. Confucius expressed my opinion about these matters when he said, "The sweat of the owner is the best fertilizer." But I am not going to say that private ownership is automatically good. Where is the owner going with his property? Toward God? or toward "splendor"?

The Book of Proverbs, part of the Bible's Wisdom Literature, points the way to the truly successful life in one sentence, "The fear of the Lord is the beginning of wisdom." In Proverbs, or Ezekiel, or in Jesus' teaching, piety is no substitute for performance. Gumption is an important ingredient in Christian life. But gumption must have a goal.

Christians ought to realize that work is sacramental, that is, an outward and visible sign of God's inward and spiritual grace. Sawing a board, steering a ship, or rocking a cradle ought to be acts of worship. These are among the ways in which we implement the divine commandment, "Love your neighbor." God blessed us with hands and gave us brains to guide them. Using our hands and minds practically by doing our work is an important part of our reasonable service to God.

The Prince of Tyre, like many other successful people, chose "splendor" as his goal, and the final result was spiritual shipwreck. Jesus asked the question that ought to burn into the heart of every ambitious person, "What shall it profit a man if he shall gain the whole world and lose his own soul?"

Ezekiel is preaching for a verdict. His congregation consists of alert, intelligent, ambitious people, whose homeland

is in ruins. They are trying to carve a new life for themselves
and their children in Babylon. What goals shall they seek?
In answer Ezekiel pictures a man who sought, and reached,
the wrong goal.

The exiles, like us, knew with their intellects that man's
only true goal is God. We can earn profits for the glory of
God, or we can earn them for our splendor. We can destroy
ourselves or find ourselves while engaged in the successful
or the unsuccessful pursuit of wealth.

Why did God give you ability? So that you can serve Him
with all your heart and with all your soul and with all your
mind and with all your strength. How do you do that?
Chiefly by loving—which means respecting—your neighbor
with the same kind of wisdom that you show in respecting
yourself.

Any economic system that puts profit ahead of justice
is in danger. I certainly do not make this as a blanket in-
dictment of our economic system. I have spent far too many
hours talking with deeply concerned, responsible business
men who are seeking the just thing in this or that dealing
with customer or employee. I know and highly respect Christian business men who are daily serving God by the effective
performance of their work. I do not condemn the system
within which they work when I point out that it, like any
other system, contains dangers, and the chief danger is that
greed may swallow justice.

Ezekiel says much the same thing. He describes a man
whose success has been the envy of the whole world—like ours
—and he says:

> By the multitude of your iniquities,
>   in the unrighteousness of your trade
>   you profaned your sanctuaries.

The Prince of Tyre had his religion, the cult of Melkarth.
Remember, Queen Jezebel imported the Tyrian faith into
Israel, where it did not shine by comparison with the faith
revealed through Abraham. Every false religion is a per-
version of the truth. The financial goals the Phoenicians set
for themselves helped to "profane their sanctuaries," and the
perverted faith encouraged them to seek the wrong goals.
What was the result?

> I brought forth fire from the midst of you:
>   it consumed you,
> and I turned you to ashes upon the earth.

This is the essential truth underlying all the complex verbiage of Karl Marx and his disciples: economics is important. Important to business, obviously, but equally important to government, culture, and spiritual life. Faith cannot ignore the economic process. And here in one sentence Ezekiel states the profound religious truth: economic greed will destroy the civilization that tolerates it.

SUCCESS TODAY

My friend, Eugene Wilson, used to be president of the United Aircraft Corporation. Years ago, he was in the Argentine on business. During one of many coffee-breaks, a gentleman from the Argentine asked him, "Why is it that you are here selling me airplanes, and I am not in New York selling them to you?" Mr. Wilson tells me that at the time he had never considered the matter, and he gave the answer that, I am almost sure, has already popped into your head. He said, "I suppose it's because we have the raw materials and you don't." I pause long enough to mention, that's the Communist answer: economic determinism. The Argentinian gentleman came as close to discourtesy as is possible for such a man. He said, "No, that is not the case. We have even more raw materials than you have." (They do.) Mr. Wilson spent several years wondering about the question, and in the process wrote several valuable books. The essence of his answer is that the North American economic system was framed by Protestant Christians.

In the third grade they told us that our founding fathers came to this country for God, and the Spanish came to Latin America for gold. This is inaccurate on two counts. Our pioneers were by no means devoid of economic motivation, and the Spaniards—many of them—were keenly interested in spiritual matters. What more evidence could you ask than the magnificent churches they built?

I rejoice that light is shining through cracks in the wall that still divides Protestant from Roman Catholic. I hope that in time the wall may crumble to the ground; so that all who love Christ may serve Him together. God know' how much we Protestants can receive from the Roman Catholics, but perhaps they can receive a few things from us. In my zeal for ecumenicity I do not intend to disown our past.

Mr. Wilson's conclusion, after years of thought, is that we inherited from our Protestant forebears a religious, economic, and political system emphasizing individual freedom from tyranny by priest or king, the individual responsibility to God that must undergird any true freedom, the sacramental value of hard work, and hope, the blazing hope that God's power will prevail. These are the principles underlined in Ezekiel, with bolder strokes, I believe, than anywhere else in the Bible.

A literary critic, whose work I read not long ago, described two fundamental life-views, the tragic and the romantic. The tragic teaches man to submit to his fate. This, of course, is the viewpoint of most modern literature, snarling submission. The romantic teaches hope and the struggle to realize one's hope, even when both the hope and the struggle seem insane. And this is Ezekiel's teaching, embodied in the culture that has produced our economic system. I had never thought of Ezekiel as a romantic figure before. And, need I say it again? We are always in danger of hoping for the wrong things and struggling for baubles.

A Christian worships God on the job, with hard work, imagination, enterprise, and all the other good qualities that the ancient Phoenicians showed in abundance. God blessed these good qualities with success, both in ancient time and today. The worship of success was the danger in ancient time, and there lies the danger today. Ezekiel's message to you is not that the ancient Tyrians had a prince named Ithobaal, but that God has a child named you, to whom He has entrusted all sorts of wonderful abilities. He gave these abilities to you because there are needs in the world, and you are the person to meet them.

The section about Tyre is one of few beautiful parts in the Prophecy of Ezekiel. Its tragic beauty is designed to aid your reflection. To help you reflect, Ezekiel shows a man with superb endowments who chooses the wrong goal for his life. From this point on the decision is yours.

At the center of their island city the Tyrians built a gigantic pillar in honor of the deity Melkarth, and, like sensible people, they put a light at the top of their tower. If the pilot steered toward the warning light, his ship would be destroyed. But if he used his nautical wisdom, the beacon would guide him into the harbor.

Ezekiel 34:2-30

Thus says the Lord God:

"Ho, shepherds of Israel who have been feeding yourselves! Should not shepherds feed the sheep? You eat the fat, you clothe yourselves with the wool, you slaughter the fatlings; but you do not feed the sheep. The weak you have not strengthened, the sick you have not healed, the crippled you have not bound up, the strayed you have not brought back, the lost you have not sought, and with force and harshness you have ruled them. So they were scattered, because there was no shepherd and they became food for all the wild beasts.... My sheep were scattered over all the face of the earth....

"Therefore ... as I live," says the Lord God ... "Behold, I am against the shepherds; and I will require my sheep at their hand....

"I, I myself will search for my sheep, and will seek them out.... I will rescue them from all places where they have been scattered on a day of clouds and thick darkness.... I will feed them on the mountains of Israel.... there they shall lie down in good grazing land, and on fat pasture they shall feed.... I myself will be the shepherd of my sheep, and I will make them lie down.... I will seek the lost, and I will bring back the strayed, and I will bind up the crippled, and I will strengthen the weak, and the fat and the strong I will watch over; I will feed them in justice.

"As for you, my flock ... Behold, I judge between sheep and sheep, rams and he-goats. Is it not enough for you to feed on the good pasture, that you must tread down with your feet the rest of your pasture; and to drink of clear water, that you must foul the rest with your feet? And must my sheep eat what you have trodden with your feet, and drink what you have fouled with your feet? ...

"Behold, I, I myself will judge between the fat sheep and the lean sheep.... I will save my flock, they shall no longer be a prey; and I will judge between sheep and sheep. And I will set up over them one shepherd, my servant David, and he shall feed them: he shall feed them and be their shepherd. And I, the Lord, will be their God, and my servant David shall be prince among them....

"I will make with them a covenant of peace and banish wild beasts from the land, so that they may dwell securely in the wilderness and sleep in the woods. And I will make them and the places round about my hill a blessing; and I will send down the showers in their season; they shall be showers of blessing. And the trees of the field shall yield their fruit, and the earth shall yield its increase, and they shall be secure in their land.... And they shall know that I, the Lord their God, am with them, and that they, the house of Israel, are my people," says the Lord God.

THE SHEPHERDS AND THE FLOCK
Ezekiel 34:2-30

The thirty-fourth chapter of Ezekiel deals with political power, as the twenty-eighth concerns economic power. Ezekiel's conclusion, you will not be greatly surprised to hear, is that political power, which is a necessary part of human life, must be directed toward God. An interesting question rises in the thoughtful reader's mind: should I consider this matter of power from the viewpoint of the shepherd or that of the sheep? Ezekiel answers it. Not only is he concerned when shepherds—mayors and governors and presidents—abuse their power, he is equally concerned when the sheep—people like you and me—make life miserable for one another. God judges the shepherd. God judges the sheep. You should read the chapter from the viewpoint of one who has precisely the amount of political power that you have.

Ezekiel belonged to the ruling class in society, yet he made the necessary effort to appreciate how it feels to be oppressed. It was not such an effort for him as it is for us. He was an exile, who had been driven from one place to another by people who cared nothing for him and his feelings. We who are comfortable and well-fed, who take political freedom for granted, find it difficult to appreciate the feelings of the poor farmer in Colombia, or the tribesman in Africa whose new-born nation stumbles while trying to walk, or the Christian mother in Budapest whose children are learning in school to despise Christ. Yet, if the Golden Rule is to be any more than religious sounding hot air, we must make the effort to see life through the other person's eyes.

THE KING OVER ISRAEL

"The powers that be are ordained of God." When Paul wrote that sentence, Nero was emperor. Certainly Paul did not mean that Nero's every action was divinely inspired. He meant that civil government is a necessary, important part of God's plan for the world. But what form of civil government? Aye, there's the rub.

In the keenest analysis yet made, Aristotle shows that three forms of civil government are possible: the monarchy, where one person rules; the democracy, where all rule; and the aristocracy, where (ideally) the few who are best qualified govern. He shows the strength and the weakness of each system, and he makes the telling point that each form of government is endangered by an excess of itself. The monarchy can degenerate into tyranny, the democracy can become the fickle impulsive mob, and the aristocracy can fritter out its life in an endless series of committee meetings. Yet it is part of God's plan for the world that His children live under some kind of civil government.

When the Children of Israel entered the Promised Land, they formed a loose tribal organization, which faced many strong enemies. A long series of Judges gave the twelve tribes what little political cohesiveness they had. We know the names of some Judges, like Samson, Eli, and Samuel. Most are not recorded in history books on earth. Those who judged faithfully are written in the Lamb's Book of Life, which is all that really counts.

The elders came to Samuel, asking, "Appoint for us a king to govern us like all the nations." The Lord said to His prophet, "They have not rejected you, but they have rejected Me." Surely the Lord is not greatly concerned about what title the ruler bears. He has blessed many nations where kings have governed. The rejection of God is not in the desire for this or that form of rule, but in the reason for seeking it. The elders who came to Samuel wanted the pomp and glory of a crown, rather than the humble walk with God.

Samuel warned the people what monarchy would mean. This does not mean that the Holy Bible is opposing one form of government. Democracies and aristocracies have fallen into the identical glory trap, as rulers have sought their own glory in preference to God's. Samuel described the oppressive monarchy the people might expect, and they clamored for it. They wanted to bask in the tawdry glory reflected from an earthly potentate. They thought they were willing to pay the price, in taxes, enforced labor, loss of individual freedom, and danger to their faith.

The people got their king, and Samuel's warning was fulfilled. Sometimes uninformed Christians talk as if the Hebrew monarchy was a glorious age of faith. They should read the Books of Samuel, Kings, and Chronicles. During four long centuries, the faith was in grave danger. Occasionally a strong, godly king, like Hezekiah, for example, would use the necessary powers of government in the way God intends. But most of the kings merely endured their faith, while a few actively opposed it.

Under King Ahab's rule, the prophet Elijah said:

> The people of Israel have forsaken thy covenant, thrown down thy altars, and slain thy prophets with the sword; and I, even I only, am left; and they seek my life, to take it away.
>
> I Kings 19:10

The Lord assured the despairing prophet that the minority was not quite so small, but still the believers were greatly outnumbered. Seven thousand faithful, plus a much larger number who were sick of the new religion and wanted to get back to what they had abandoned, and one fiery prophet were God's human resources to overcome the evils wrought by a king who abused his divinely given power.

Ezekiel gloomily makes it clear that his people will not require a king when they return to their own land. For centuries after the return, the little country, Palestine, was one of few that were governed without a king. As a usual thing, the High Priest took over the necessary, important duties of the civil ruler. After the revolt against the Greeks, royal powers were given to the Maccabean family, but the title, King, was withheld until the days when John Hyrcanus usurped it, about a century and a quarter before Jesus' time.

I have never enthused about the method of Bible teaching under which innocent children are asked to memorize the kings of Judah and Israel. The Bible is not about them, it is about God. The words of praise or condemnation for earthly rulers are for our guidance in the moral situations where we are.

THE RESPONSIBILITY OF POWER

We who live under political freedom, who elect our rulers, bear a responsibility that we cannot transfer. As soon as we seek to achieve desirable goals through the right exercise of our political power, we discover that the way is complex and filled with difficulties. Come to think of it, that's exactly what King Hezekiah discovered. Remember, we who vote are the governing class. As he describes the shepherds and their responsibility, Ezekiel is not talking about Hezekiah and Ahab; he is talking about us.

"Ho, shepherds of Israel who have been feeding yourselves! Should not shepherds feed the sheep?" Ezekiel had the unfortunate habit of making his points negatively. The point is still quite pointed. We who enjoy political power must be concerned about those who are powerless. With all the checks and restraints that our country has developed, we still have smarted under petty tyranny from petty officials, and we have known some major tyrannizing by political bosses and others who have sought the rewards of power and have corrupted its responsibilities. Yet these things glare out simply because we have accepted the idea of the "public servant."

The public servant concept has never been more tellingly expressed than in *A Bell for Adano*. Major Joppolo, commanding the occupation forces, is speaking to the village officials, most of whom learned their trade under fascism. Although they are mature, intelligent people, the Major addresses them as if they were children; for he is introducing a concept that is simple to state and difficult to grasp.

> Democracy is that the men of the government are no longer masters of the people. They are the servants of the people. What makes a man master of another man? It is that he pays him for his work. Who pays the men in the government? The people do, for they pay the taxes out of which you are paid. Therefore, you are now the servants of the people of Adano. . . . You must behave now as servants, not as masters. . . . And watch: this thing will make you happier than you have ever been in your lives.

The public servant has power and authority because these

are necessary for him to carry out his responsibility. They are not luxuries to be enjoyed, but sharp edged tools, to be kept and used for the public good. Quite rightly, we expect our elected and appointed officials to consider themselves public servants. But how about us who elect? How should we think of ourselves? If we are Christian, we will recognize that we are here to serve, while we vote and all the rest of the time.

Continuing his unfortunate habit of stating positive truth negatively, Ezekiel delineates the civil magistrate's duty. For us who live in political freedom, this means our duty to vote for the kind of people who will carry out these responsibilities, and to support the policies that will make them possible.

> The weak you have not strengthened, the sick you have not healed, the crippled you have not bound up, the strayed you have not brought back, the lost you have not sought, and with force and harshness you have ruled them.

The first task of civil government is to provide order, within which people can go peaceably about their affairs. I find it extremely interesting that Ezekiel does not suggest, here or elsewhere, that government should manage business or agriculture. Business men and farmers, by and large, do a much better job of it. But always, in ever society, some fall by the wayside. Some are not able to fend for themselves. Society is responsible to care for these who cannot care for themselves: the crippled, the sick, the weak.

We in the United States ought to wince when God's holy Word vividly describes our responsibility, through our officials, to bring back the strayed and to seek the lost. Never mind the group in ancient society to which Ezekiel referred. His words smart if we apply them to ourselves. And if we don't, then we are misusing the Bible. We have quite a few lost and strayed persons in our own country. Do we really care about them?

By any meaningful definition, a convicted criminal is badly strayed or lost. Our government, which contains much that is wonderfully good, seems willing to dwell in the darkest of dark ages when it comes to treating him like a man. Our Federal Penitentiaries are the least bad in this respect. Most of the State Penitentiaries are awful. And the County and

City Jails are a disgrace. When a person is accused of a crime, we assume his innocence until guilt is proved beyond the shadow of a doubt. If he cannot afford legal counsel, we provide a skillful attorney to plead his case. We move mountains to assure that he receives a just trial. I do not pretend that we perfectly succeed. No people ever have perfectly succeeded. But up to the moment of conviction, we recognize the accused as a fellow human being. The minute he is convicted, we throw him into a cell and let him rot.

Some few enlightened wardens, with miserable budgets, are doing their best to make a convict's prison sentence a time of rehabilitation rather than a graduate school in crime. Underpaid psychologists and psychiatrists are striving to bring scientific healing to warped personalities. Devoted prison chaplains, struggling against mountains of public apathy, are seeking all and reaching a few of the lost. Praise and thanks to those who, each in his own way, are trying to implement what Ezekiel says about the duty of government. But when the praise and thanks have been rendered, the cruel fact remains that we in the United States are wallowing along with penal attitudes and procedures that were out of date a century ago. We cannot blame the legislators and the governors, much less the wardens. We, the shepherds, have been so busy feeding ourselves that we have not been concerned about the lost sheep.

Naturally, our first concern with a criminal should be preventive. The best time to stop a crime wave is before it becomes a ripple. Why do people stray morally? Why are they lost? I have talked with hundreds of convicted criminals, and every time one of them has opened up enough for me to look inside his soul—it happens more often than you might think—I have found a large, God-shaped emptiness.

My respectable friends—of whom I still have a few—seem surprised when I say that my friends on the outer edge of society have much the same kind of needs and feelings that any one else has. Every man's central need is a living faith in God. When this is lacking, people fill the gap as well as they can. The majority fill it in ways that are socially acceptable. The rapidly growing minority fill it in other ways.

For the past ten years I have been receiving the annual

report on crime published by the Federal Bureau of Investigation, which makes fascinating, if not uplifting, reading material. I quote from the report that happens to be closest on my shelf. Any other in the ten year period would say the same thing, with a slight change in percentage points.

> Crime in the United States as measured by the Crime Index was 19% higher during the first 3 months of 19.. than the first quarter of 19... Nationally, increases were recorded in all offenses, led by property crimes, with auto theft up 22%, larceny over 21%, and both burglary and robbery up 19%. Crimes against the person also showed sharp increases.

Apparently the shepherds of Israel have been doing less than an ideal job. And who are the shepherds? Certainly not the President. Certainly not the Governor. Certainly not the Director of the F.B.I. It's you and me Ezekiel is talking about.

GOD IS IN COMMAND OF HISTORY

Ezekiel and his congregation were enduring the result of abused political power. Remember, political means how organized society acts. It has no necessary connection with smoke-filled rooms and the other juvenile apparatus of democracy. Where is this society? Where is it going? And how does it plan to get there? These are the essential political questions.

Ezekiel's society had perversely sought the wrong goals. The result was long in coming, but it came.

> They were scattered, because there was no shepherd, and they became food for all the wild beasts.... My sheep were scattered over all the face of the earth.

The abuse of any good thing leads inevitably to a disastrous result. Sometimes the destruction is outward and visible—as with the exiles—sometimes it is inward and spiritual.

Our faith concerns what God is doing to restore what man has destroyed. And surely you noticed one word in the quotation above, which makes all the difference between despair and hope. The battered, troubled people, who have suffered from indifferent and greedy shepherds, are *my* sheep. The other Son of Man says much the same thing in His vivid and awesome picture of the Judgment. He pictures His friends showing intelligent concern for the refugee, the migrant, the penniless victim of flood or hurricane, and the jailbird. He says, "As you did it to one of the least of these, my brethren, you did it to me." God cares about people. He cares about prosperous, well-dressed people. He likewise cares about the share-cropper, the unemployed miner, the alcoholic, and the convict.

We who have privilege are supposed to use it for the benefit of those who have none. When we fail to do so, the result may be long delayed, but it will come.

> Behold I am against the shepherds; and I will require my sheep at their hand . . . no longer shall the shepherds feed themselves. I will rescue my sheep from their mouths.

Those who abuse political power will lose it. God is in charge of history. His judgment often is long delayed, but He judges. People who did not know God as revealed to Abraham and Moses coined a proverb: "The mills of God grind slow, but they grind exceeding fine." Neither God's friends nor His enemies can afford to ignore that divine justice operates in the world.

Ezekiel's congregation had nothing to hope for. The throne on which their king once reigned had, quite possibly, been carted off to the royal museum in Babylon, where a snickering attendant would show it to any one who cared to look. Their puny kingdom was destroyed and their spiritual aspirations with it. Nebuchadnezzar and his mighty army were in charge of history. There was nothing on which to base any intelligent hope. Nothing means "no thing." But a power reigns above and beyond this world of things, where political counsels go askew and banks fail and immaculate hospitals are suddenly filled with streptococcus infection.

The Lord says about His children who have no thing on which to base their hope:

> I will rescue them from all places where they have been scattered on a day of clouds and thick darkness.

We who look to God do not base our trust upon things, good and necessary things that God made for our use and final salvation, we trust God, who was in charge of ancient history, and is in charge of history today.

We have been examining the chapter from the viewpoint

of the shepherds. We who enjoy political freedom are "shepherds" who bear heavy responsibility. Let's think now from the viewpoint of the sheep. We have, after all, received troubles as well as inflicted them. Often enough, with the best intentions in the world, we do not know what is the right thing to do, and we receive an unending supply of contradictory advice. We are bewildered. We feel lost. And the Lord says to us:

> I will seek the lost, and I will bring back the strayed, and I will bind up the crippled, and I will strengthen the weak, and the fat and the strong I will watch over; I will feed them in justice.

If you will look at the small footnote in your Bible, you will see one of the many difficult puzzles the translator of Ezekiel must attempt to solve. Some early manuscripts read "The fat and the strong I will watch over." Other manuscripts read, "The fat and the strong I will destroy." In this case I am almost certain that Ezekiel wrote, "I will watch over." You can appreciate how a scribe, at some painful juncture in history, smarting under the injustice of a local tyrant, changed the word to destroy. But neither Ezekiel nor anyone else who thinks seriously wishes to see strength destroyed. Strength dedicated: that's what Ezekiel is after. Your strength.

Jesus took Ezekiel's beautiful picture of the shepherd and the sheep—God's sheep—and based some of His most beloved parables upon it. And, as He frequently did, Jesus went beyond Ezekiel's teaching. Remember, Ezekiel has gone much farther than many people today, who seem to think of God as the divine Conundrum. Ezekiel—just as puzzled as we are by daily events—sees God seeking the lost, bringing back the strayed, binding up the crippled, strengthening the weak, and watching over the strong. The laboratory demonstration for this victory was the return to Jerusalem. The other Son of Man, looking to the ultimate victory, says, "I lay down my life for the sheep." And His laboratory demonstration was the Resurrection. I am not being irreverent or flippant about the Resurrection or the return to Jerusalem. A laboratory is a place where a person labors. These two events took place in this world where we labor, and they demonstrate that God labors here too.

THE END OF THE ROAD

I have said that the really important political questions are: Where are we? Where are we going? and, How do we plan to get there? The lines of our present political conflict are becoming dimly visible, on a world-wide scale. Some answer these questions in temporal aspiration, some in eternal. We should not facilely decide that the democracies are always in the right and the dictatorships always in the wrong. Within our country we have many who do not give a hoot about eternity, and in the lands where the rulers profess to despise God, millions still have not bowed the knee to Baal.

We think about the choice between time and eternity as a religious question. It is likewise the central political question of our time. Ezekiel tells us over and over again that our politics and our faith must have a considerable overlap, if either is to achieve its intended purpose. Rephrase the political question this way: Are justice and human dignity merely convenient rules of the road that we have decided to adopt and can change when they are inconvenient, or are these qualities written into the unchanging constitution of things so that we must adjust our government and everything else to them?

Brilliant people are upholding alternative philosophies today. We can label one philosophy as humanism, the other as faith. The labels are imperfect, because humanism is a faith, and faith is all in favor of anything that genuinely will benefit human beings, but for rough and ready purposes, the labels can stand. If the central political questions deal with where you are, where you are going, and how you plan to get there, then you ought to ask these questions from each alternative.

What does humanism offer? The humanist considers himself part of the natural world. He asks his followers for hard work, dedication, self-sacrifice, and all the rest that goes with human effort. The humanists show precious little agreement about the road we should follow, but they affirm loudly, if not always convincingly, that if we will only scrap the state, or deify the state, or nationalize industry, or get government out of business, then things will be much better than they are now. The best of the humanists, like Bertrand Russell, for instance, do not think of "better" in merely physical terms. They are passionately concerned with righteousness, justice, and peace.

Mr. Russell dedicated a long, productive life to the humanist gospel. When he was about eighty years old, he wrote an important, brief essay, *Can Scientific Man Survive?* His concluding words are:

> [Human survival] demands a morality which will be new only in the sense of being acted upon. As an ideal, it is not new, but very old. It has been preached for countless centuries by sages and religious leaders, who have been highly honored after being put to death. I hope, though not with complete confidence, that men may learn to permit themselves to be happy, even at the cost of enduring the happiness of those whom they have hitherto hated. If this lesson can be learnt in time, science can lay the foundation of a new Golden Age. If it cannot be learnt, every increase of knowledge will be only a step towards ultimate and complete disaster.

I find this a bewildering statement. I am familiar with illogical thinking. I hear it all the time, and do some of it myself. But Mr. Russell is the outstanding logician of modern time, and here he says that if we will only build upon spiritual foundations, then human striving can build firm foundations for a better life. We who believe in the way of faith insist upon the need for human striving. But now Mr. Russell tells us that the thing he has been passionately recommending is insufficient without the thing we have been talking about all along.

Unless we build upon spiritual foundations, Mr. Russell warns, we shall incur inevitable disaster. He is quite correct. But suppose the human race manages somehow to tolerate itself while forgetting its Creator. Suppose people manage to stagger from crisis to crisis, with God increasingly in the past tense. What then? Aldous Huxley's brilliant book, *Brave New World,* is an honest answer to the question. And to me it is a far more devastating picture of hell than anything Dante ever wrote.

Suppose Mr. Huxley is wrong, and finally people will learn

how to live with one another, without reference to God. What then? The humanist cries, "Don't bother us with ultimates. We have enough troubles now." The end of the road is a cosmic accident, a change in the temperature of the sun, a genetic mutation, a new and unconquerable virus—and the dark.

What does faith promise? Ezekiel, the master of symbolism pictures the end of man's long journey in symbols of a simple, agricultural society. He pictures the Children of Israel returned to the Promised Land, where God will "banish wild beasts from the land, so that they may dwell securely in the wilderness and sleep in the woods." Further, the Lord promises, "I will send down showers in their season; they shall be showers of blessing." This last expression, "showers of blessing," is one of very few expressions from Ezekiel that have entered Christian devotional language. After security and rainfall will come fertility. "The trees of the field shall yield their fruit, and the earth shall yield its increase, and they shall be secure in their land."

The farmer in central Florida has achieved all that Ezekiel here promises, if you look merely at the symbol. He knows abundant rainfall. His trees are loaded with fruit. And he must go to the zoo to see any wild animals. Yet, if you have any serious contact with the farmers of our state you know well that we have not reached the end of the road. Ezekiel uses material symbols to describe man's true goal in life. "They shall know that I, the Lord their God, am with them, and that they, the house of Israel, are my people, says the Lord God."

I mentioned the two starting points. We can begin with ourselves, or we can begin with God. The two journeys involve struggle and toil, with frequent tears and occasional laughter. The one offers tantalizing visions of material plenty, and then the dark. The other warns that the way of faith may lead to a cross, and then to eternal light and life.

Once I was talking with a professional cynic who said, "What's all this talk about eternal life? I think it's the most awful thing you could possibly offer anyone. At least I have the comfort of knowing that one day it will all be ended. But you tell people that their lives will drag on forever.

It's just plain hell." And, for once, the cynic was quite right. If our faith offered nothing more than continued existence after physical death, I would not be greatly interested in proclaiming or even believing such depressing news. When Jesus says, "I am the resurrection and the life," He offers a new quality of being, not just dragging on and on, but perfect consciousness of God's presence. Ezekiel described it, "They shall know that I, the Lord their God, am with them, and that they, the house of Israel, are my people, says the Lord God." This is the end of the road, for the man of faith. And it's worth all the struggle it takes to get there.

Ezekiel 37:1-10

The hand of the Lord was upon me, and he brought me out by the Spirit of the Lord, and set me down in the midst of the valley; and it was full of bones. And he led me round among them; and behold, there were very many upon the valley; and lo, they were very dry. And he said to me, "Son of man, can these bones live?" And I answered, "O Lord God, thou knowest." Again he said to me, "Prophesy to these bones, and say to them, O dry bones, hear the word of the Lord. Thus says the Lord God to these bones: Behold, I will cause breath to enter you, and you shall live. And I will lay sinews upon you, and will cause flesh to come upon you, and cover you with skin, and put breath in you, and you shall live; and you shall know that I am the Lord."

So I prophesied as I was commanded; and as I prophesied, there was a noise, and behold, a rattling; and the bones came together, bone to its bone. And as I looked, there were sinews on them, and flesh had come upon them, and skin had covered them; but there was no breath in them. Then he said to me, "Prophesy to the breath, prophesy, Son of man, and say to the breath, Thus saith the Lord God: Come from the four winds, O breath, and breathe upon these slain, that they may live." So I prophesied as he commanded me, and the breath came into them, and they lived, and stood upon their feet, an exceedingly great host.

THE DIFFERENCE THE SPIRIT MAKES
Ezekiel 37:1-10

In a vision the lonely prophet was led to a battlefield where his people had suffered a massive defeat. To his left were the dried, bleached bones of soldiers who had fallen. To his right were bones. Before him and behind him were bones. No motion, no life, just bones. These bones symbolize that the people whom Ezekiel loved were spiritually dead, and that his discouragement fell little short of total despair. For twenty-five centuries now, people discouraged for any valid reason have been finding courage in Ezekiel's weird report of despair that the Holy Spirit transformed into hope.

ARE THINGS REALLY SO BAD?

Spiritual death is a figure of speech, not a medical report. A person who is spiritually dead may be abounding in physical health and energy. He may be intellectually brilliant and he may be successful in his business life. The late Al Capone was among the outstanding organizers and administrators in American history. He became a wealthy, powerful man. As far as I am aware, he was in good physical health during the days of his major achievement. Yet almost anybody would agree that spiritually he was in bad shape.

It is distressing how often sincere Christians have been estranged from one another by figures of speech. The Calvinists and the Arminians for the past few centuries have been disagreeing, sometimes at the top of their lungs. The two doctors look at the patient, man. Dr. Arminian says, "He is desperately sick. He belongs on the critical list. Without the life-giving Spirit of Christ he is lost." Dr. Calvinist says, "Sick, nothing, he is dead. Only Christ can restore him to life." Had the energy expended by Calvinists and Arminians in attacking each other's language been directed toward reviving the patient, Ezekiel's eerie vision might not seem quite so depressingly homelike to Methodist and Presbyterian clergymen today.

Spiritual death is a figure of speech. Don't press it too far. No person living on earth today is totally beyond the reach of divine love. God calls to the worst in the human population. The miracle of faith still works to transform extortioners and call-girls. Before they answered the call of Christ, you might say that spirtually they were dying or they were dead. Does it make much difference which figure of speech you use? What matters is the love of Christ that brings them to life.

When I talk about someone who is spirtually dead, or sick if you prefer the expression, I mean someone who has no genuine basis for hope unless he responds to the Spirit of God. I have thus described Al Capone, extortionists and call-girls, all of whom were created in the image of God, and then abused their divine gift of life in one way or another. And so, we decide complacently, that lets me off the hook. I'm not like that.

Neither were the people to whom Ezekiel was talking. They were Hebrew exiles, far from the land they loved. Their homes were destroyed, and their Temple lay in ruins, but they were doing fairly well at that. Archaeologists have been grubbing among the ruins and they have reconstructed a fairly comfortable life for the Hebrew refugees who were located in settlements not far from the city of Babylon. Skilled workers practiced their trades. Many engaged in truck gardening to supply the city's unending hunger. Some opened stores. Not many years later one of the principle banks in the Babylonian empire was run by a Hebrew family. Perhaps at the time Ezekiel saw his strange vision the family had already begun a small money-lending business.

The Hebrew people have shown an uncanny ability to survive under difficult circumstances. In Babylonia they survived. They were adjusting quite nicely. And this is what Ezekiel is disturbed about. What were they adjusting to? And what would happen to their spiritual life if they adjusted to it? He was trying to enlist soldiers in the army of the Lord. His potential recruits, he decided, were smug suburbanites, more interested in comfort than in taking a stand for God. They were self-satisfied and inclined to leave well enough alone. But were they spiritually dead?

You can say two things about the exiles and their spiritual health. First, they were not on fire with the Spirit. If you had asked, they would have told you, with a resigned shrug of the shoulders, that they believed in God. Then you must add that they lived without hope. Oh, naturally, Solomon hoped to buy a new yoke of oxen, and Isaac hoped to make a good profit in selling a young camel. They had that sort of hope, just the way Al Capone hoped to consolidate the vice-rings of Cook County. But the hope that one's individual life could be a significant contribution to God's victory on earth — that hope was dead. What's the use of the moral struggle? That and a dime will buy you a cup of coffee. The exiles were bitter and cynical about God. Faith? Be practical, man. Repentance? Something our fathers did. Hope? Don't be a fool.

Now let's look around our neighborhood. Here's a man who is holding down a responsible position. He is earning a large salary. He lives in a lovely home and he drives a good car. He has never been near a jail. He has never been involved in a scandal. He does not drink to excess. He does not use narcotics. And he is faithful to his wife. Once, long ago, he made a profession of faith in Jesus Christ. Today, he will tell you with a quiet, disarming smile, "I think religion is good for the kiddies." When the Holy Bible tells us that such a man is spirtually dead, we recoil in horror and say, "But he's such a *nice* person."

Ezekiel described his friends and neighbors as a collection of dry bones, and he was talking about nice successful people whose faith was fizzling out.

Now perhaps we have thought enough about other people's spiritual health. There is one person for whose spiritual life you are uniquely responsible. Is that person spiritually alive? Remember, we are measuring by God's standard, not the community's. The community is satisfied if you perform the duties of citizenship fairly well. God asks, "Are you born again?" He is not nearly so concerned with your present attainments as He is with the direction of your growth.

Are other people seeing in you what a Christian life ought to be? Every member of this congregation has promised God and the rest of us that he will share faithfully in the worship and service of the Church. Other people can see whether or not you are keeping this promise. What do they see?

We are always using the financial yardstick the wrong way; maybe once in a while we might use it correctly. I knew a man who was strictly a nobody until, in the fifty-third year of his life, he inherited a large and unexpected bequest. Then of a sudden his opinions became important and his jokes funny. This, I submit, is the wrong way to use the financial yardstick. The right way? What percentage of your income is invested in the Kingdom of God?

Do I need to remind you that a person can make a splendid holy show and miss the whole point of what faith is about? It is no accident that Jesus saved His sternest condemnation for the sins of religious people. They were called scribes and Pharisees in His day. Today we call them Presbyterians and Pentecostals and Episcopalians. Others can see when you bow your head. Nobody but you can know whether or not you are praying. Self-examination is something that only you can do. Only you can repent. Only you can receive God's forgiveness.

When you united with this congregation, you pledged to "give your whole heart to Christ and His Kingdom." With your lips you made the promise. Are there still a few corners of your heart where Christ is not exactly welcome?

Jesus said, "Love your neighbor." Our country is going through heart-rending struggle because many of our Negro neighbors believe that their white neighbors do not love them. If they are correct, this is tragic in a land where sixty per cent of the people claim to be Christian. I speak with full awareness that some Negroes are lazy, immoral, diseased, ignorant, and irresponsible. (So are some white people.) The Lord who commanded us all to love our neighbor gave some of us special privileges and advantages; just so that we would be in a position to make Christian love effective among the people who need it most. Yet a good many of us who are privileged would be delighted if Jesus would stay away from the corner of our hearts marked "race-relations."

And here we are back, jarringly, in the Valley of Dry Bones. This is the embarrassing thing about the Son of Man. We were comfortably talking about someone else — exiles or racketeers or Pharisees — and all of a sudden, if we interpret the prophecy with the slightest honesty, we find ourselves looking in a mirror.

Am I spiritually dead? Take the Spirit of Christ away from my life, and what would be left? A biological organism that functions reasonably well. I suppose without faith in Christ I would keep on eating and sleeping. I might be tolerably successful at earning a living. I probably would not commit any major crimes, or if I did, I like to think I'm smart enough that I wouldn't get caught. But without Christ, what hope would I have? A bigger car? A swimming pool? A cabin cruiser? A three-month vacation every winter? Yes, this kind of cultivated mammalian hope that is just the human version of a dog's hope for a large bone or a horse's hope that the flies will go away.

Without the Spirit could I realistically hope for peace on earth and understanding among the nations? Could I reasonably hope that God will "crown our good with brotherhood?" Could I hope that my puny efforts actually count in the battle betwixt good and evil? Without God could I hold to any genuine hope that is worthy of a human being?

The cynical sneer is the mark of our time. It was the mark of Ezekiel's time. As he watched his neighbors growing increasingly cynical about God and their faith, absorbing more and more of their energy in the scramble for profits, Ezekiel described them as a valley of dry bones.

Change the figure of speech if you want to. But face the question as honestly as you can: "Where, but in the divine Spirit, can I hope?"

THE WRONG PLACES TO LOOK FOR LIFE

When you look at another person, you cannot tell whether he is spiritually alive or dead. Only God can do that. Jesus said to some pious folk that many harlots were closer to the Kingdom of God than they were. A person who is weak and knows it is stronger than the weak person who thinks he is strong.

A person may lack every outward advantage of background and upbringing and still be heading, in ways invisible to us, toward the life Christ planned. A person may have every advantage of background and upbringing, he may live an outwardly serene and virtuous life, and he may be missing the goal completely.

It sounds old-fashioned to talk about a goal. It is stylish today — though the style seem to be on the wane — to chant, "There are no Absolutes." If we throw away the Absolute — really I prefer the term God — we still find that we must aim our lives somewhere; so we set up goals for our striving. Quite likely these are reasonable and sensible goals, if we consider them over-night lodgings on the way to the city whose builder and maker is God.

The trouble comes when we pin our hope to things. This is the essential sin of idolatry. The prophets of old were not incensed about the religious use of statuary, but about the thought underlying idol-worship. An idol is a power of nature or of human culture that men elevate and say, "This is my god. This is the goal for my life. This is what I will strive to reach. Here lies my hope."

What are our idols today? I think the chief among them are prosperity, technological advance, education, and military security. Each one of these is good and necessary. If there is to be spirtual life, there must be economic production and distribution. Human needs cry for technological fulfillment. There must be people who know enough to deal with the problems we face. And there must be a civil order. So the teacher, the merchant, the scientist, and the soldier can all be servants of God. Can we pin our hope to them and their efforts? Germany was the most highly educated and most technically advanced nation on earth when Adolph Hitler came to power. Prosperity is an elusive thing, as everyone knows whose memory goes back to 1929. And the two words "Maginot Line" should remind us that it is disastrous folly to put our "trust in reeking tube and iron shard."

I listen to the radio, or sit with my eyes more or less glued to the television screen, while profound thinkers analyze the ills of our time. I read books and magazine articles about what's wrong with the world. Somewhere, in all the dark

cloud the analysts are dissecting so skillfully, there must be
a wee flicker of light. If it's there, I can't see it. The econo-
mists plan and produce a higher standard of living. The military leaders seek and find deadlier and yet deadlier weapons.
The scientists and engineers imagine and then produce miracles by the dozen. And our colleges are getting bigger all of
the time. But where is the hope?

Sometimes we forget that the end result of our planning
and producing and defending is supposed to be the life and
liberty of people. Are the people you talk with genuinely
free? Free, for instance, from destructive tension? Has our
magnificent material advance led to stable, enduring mar-
riages? Our young people have a standard of luxury that
young people never before have known anywhere. Is there
perhaps something just a little wrong when increasing numbers of them are flaunting their sexual promiscuity, are using
marijuana and other narcotics, and are engaging in flagrant
and violent crime? I have talked with youngsters thirteen,
fifteen, seventeen years old, from good, or at least prosperous
homes, who were convicted of burglary, rape, or murder. Why
did they do it? "The kicks, man, the kicks."

Is there, perhaps, something missing from modern life?
Can we increase our spirtual security by building another
nuclear submarine? or adding another couple of billion to
the Gross National Product? or starting more universities? or
even landing a few hardy souls on the planet Mars? Our
society has pinned its hope in the wrong places. If we have
no resource other than our own wits, there is no hope.

Our situation resembles that which Ezekiel faced. The people about him had material plenty. They had their private,
individual goals for life: a larger garden, an ox-cart to transport vegetables to the market, a better stall in the brass-
market, a new bookkeeper for the bank. These things are
necessary parts of spiritual life. But when a man's goal in
society can be summed up by the word "more," that man is
spiritually sick. You might as well describe him, in spiritual
terms, as a bundle of dry bones.

THE SOURCE OF OUR HOPE

Where is Ezekiel's hope? For thirty-six chapters we have
been exploring the human situation with him. We have found

weak people confronted with decisions too big for them. But we have found something else. Ezekiel, a man dominated by the Spirit, teaches us to put our hope for the future in the Spirit.

What do we mean by spirit? The other day when I looked up the word in my dictionary, I was surprised to find that it has twenty-two meanings. First we eliminate those that don't apply to this discussion: spirit means "spook" for instance, and it likewise means "alcohol," which will not help us much in our understanding Ezekiel.

The word first meant wind or air. From that inevitably it came to mean breath. It was another natural step to the sort of activity where a person's breath comes in sharp, jagged gasps. A spirited game, for instance, is one where the players give their utmost energy. A spirited debate is filled with earnestness that barely falls short of anger. A person who is in good spirits is almost breathless with excitement. So the word came to take in many attitudes of human personality.

A person can have a generous, kind, thoughtful and gracious spirit. He can also be in low spirits. I suppose people would understand if you said that someone had a mean, nasty, greedy spirit, but I have seldom heard the word used in that sense. The word embraces all of our moods, especially the nobler ones. School spirit means loyalty. Our language has no word to describe the lack of such loyalty. All we can say is that the students demonstrate no school spirit.

The spirit of a message is the meaning that lies underneath all the polished or rough-hewn phrases. The spirit of an assembly is the agreement for which the speakers could not find adequate words.

In sum, the spirit of a thing is its essence, what remains when you have taken away everything unimportant. And so your spirit means the real, essential you. Sometimes we call this reality your consciousness, or your personality, or your soul. Not surprisingly, people in many lands have called the invisible reality behind the seen world by the name they use for human personality. Beyond all its earthly meanings Spirit means God.

The word spirit comes to us from the Latin *spiritus*. It entered our language with almost all the rich context that I have been describing. But something strange and almost beyond explanation happened many centuries ago. Among the Semitic peoples of the Near East an odd-sounding word, *ruach,* was going through almost the same gamut of meanings. Different people, with different cultures, under different skies, speaking different languages used different words in almost exactly the same sense. I could just as easily have taken you on a tour through the Old Testament, where we would have found the word *ruach* (really, you're supposed to clear your throat at the end of it) meaning energy and loyalty and bubbling enthusiasm, everything that makes a person an interesting, attractive person; and wind, air, or breath; and God.

Let me read you the prophecy, substituting the original word for the several translations:

> And he said to me, "Son of man, can these bones live?"
> And I answered, "O Lord God, thou knowest."
> Again he said to me, "Prophesy to these bones, and say to them, O dry bones, hear the word of the Lord."
> Thus says the Lord God to these bones: "Behold, I will cause *ruach* to enter you, and you shall live. And I will lay sinews upon you, and will cause flesh to come upon you, and cover you with skin, and put *ruach* in you, and you shall live; and you shall know that I am the Lord."
> So I prophesied as I was commanded; and as I prophesied, there was a noise, and behold, a rattling; and the bones came together bone to its bone. And as I looked, there were sinews on them, and flesh had come upon them, and skin had covered them, but there was no *ruach* in them.
> Then he said to me, "Prophesy to the *ruach*, prophesy Son of man, and say to the *ruach*, thus says the Lord God: Come from the four *ruchoth* [that's the plural of *ruach*], O *ruach*, and breathe upon these slain, that they may live."
> So I prophesized as he commanded me, and the *ruach* came into them, and they lived, and stood upon their feet, an exceedingly great host.

Now do you see what the thirty-seventh chapter of Ezekiel is about? Here are people who have lost all sense of spiritual direction. They have their little private individual goals, worthy enough in their way, but as individuals and as a nation they are not seeking man's true goal. They have forgotten where to look. And the prophet reminds them of the power that man did not create and man cannot destroy: the Spirit of the living God. The Spirit will carry out the divine purpose despite the hostility of His enemies, and more important, despite the lethargy of His friends. What God has begun, God will finish. Will you work with Him today?

When I read Ezekiel's report of his eerie vision, I hope that a small bell rang in the back of your mind, "I've heard that somewhere else." Yes, you have. The other Son of Man took Ezekiel 37 and incorporated it into one of His most beloved teachings. This is written up in the Gospel where John uses the Greek word *pneuma*, that has come into English as pneumatic. Here in another language and another culture, a sound made in the human voice-box came to embrace almost the same meanings that we have found in English, Latin, and Hebrew. Here is the same play on meanings of wind—you—God, all wrapped up in the word *pneuma*.

> Nicodemus said to him, "How can a man be born again when he is old? Can he enter a second time into his mother's womb and be born?"
>
> Jesus answered, "Truly, truly, I say to you, unless one is born of water and the *pneuma*, he cannot enter the kingdom of God. That which is born of the flesh is flesh, and that which is born of the *pneuma* is *pneuma*. Do not marvel that I said to you, 'You must be born anew.' The *pneuma* blows where it wills, and you hear the sound of it, but you do not know whence it comes or wither it goes; so it is with every one who is born of the *pneuma*.

Both Ezekiel and Jesus were speaking to the imagination, using picturesque figures of speech and bold plays on the meaning of a word. Both were in earnest. Both were speaking to cultivated, intelligent, successful people who believed in God and were making good money. What more could anyone ask? Ezekiel says, "Without the Spirit of God, you are spiritually dead." Jesus says, "You can be born again through the Holy Spirit."

When the Spirit had finished his work, the dead bones formed "an exceedingly great host." They were an army ready for battle. Can you, with a straight face, describe yourself as a soldier in the Lord's army? Have you put on the whole armor of God? Or is your faith a private luxury to provide you with a little peace of mind in a troubled world? Is your Church membership an attack on life or a refuge from life?

In your baptism you were enlisted in the army of Christ.

What sort of performance-rating have you earned? A soldier goes to the danger spots, where his Captain sends him. He goes at risk of his life to places he doesn't want to be, to do things he doesn't want to do. And this is a test of spiritual life, that only you can apply to yourself. Who is in charge of your decisions? You or Christ? If you are, then Ezekiel is telling you that you need to submit yourself fully, completely, to the Spirit of God. If Christ is in charge of your decisions, then you are spiritually alive. You may have a long way to go before you reach the goal, but you are heading in the right direction.

Ezekiel 38:3-23

Thus says the Lord God: "Behold, I am against you, O Gog, chief prince of Meshech and Tubal; and I will turn you about, and put hooks into your jaws, and I will bring you forth, and all your army, horses and horsemen, all of them clothed in full armor, a great company, all of them with buckler and shield, wielding swords. . . .

"After many days you will be mustered; in the latter years you will go against the land that is restored from war . . . which had been a continual waste; its people were brought out from the nations and now dwell securely, all of them. You will advance, coming on like a storm, you will be like a cloud covering the land, you and all your hordes, and many peoples with you. . . .

"On that day thoughts will come into your mind, and you will devise an evil scheme and say, 'I will go up against the land of unwalled villages; I will fall upon the quiet people who dwell securely, all of them dwelling without walls, and having no bars or gates'; to seize spoil and carry off plunder. . . .

"In the latter days I will bring you against my land, that the nations may know me, when through you, O Gog, I vindicate my holiness before their eyes. . . .

"On that day there shall be a great shaking in the land of Israel; the fish of the sea, and the birds of the air, and the beasts of the field, and all creeping things that creep on the ground, and all the men that are upon the face of the earth, shall quake at my presence, and the mountains shall be thrown down, and the cliffs shall fall, and every wall shall tumble to the ground. I will summon every kind of terror against Gog" says the Lord God. . . . "With pestilence and bloodshed I will enter into judgment with him; and I will rain upon him and his hordes and the many peoples that are with him, torrential rains and hailstones, fire and brimstone. So I will show my greatness and my holiness and make myself known in the eyes of many nations. Then they will know that I am the Lord."

GOD'S PROVIDENCE
Ezekiel 38:3-23

Take a quick look at the ground-plan of Ezekiel's prophecy. After all, he is the one who taught us to think nobly about God by looking at an architectural drawing. The first twenty-four chapters in his book are filled with the tragic message that Jerusalem must fall before Nebuchadnezzar. (It did.) The latter half is filled with the glorious message that Jerusalem will live again, and the smoke will rise once more from the altar of God. (And that happened, too.) Chapters 25-32 tell us that God is in charge of all nations, from insignificant Edom to haughty Egypt. Chapters 33-37 say that the exiles will return. Chapters 40-48 show the glory of God guiding a redeemed people and filling their lives with grace, mercy, and peace.

What can we make of Chapters 38-39? They just don't fit into the picture. The last word in Chapter 37 was "forevermore." Here was Israel living at peace. The people were quietly going about their business, the priests were serving the Lord in the Temple, and the farmers serving Him behind their plows. Then in Chapter 38 Gog — whoever he is — comes from Magog — wherever that is — with a huge destructive army. There is a hideous battle and Gog is defeated. It just doesn't add up. Or does it?

WHAT KIND OF WRITING IS THIS?

Whenever you encounter a piece of writing, in the Bible or anywhere else, you must stop and ask yourself just what sort of writing it is. The process is almost automatic, when we are reading anything except the Holy Bible. Compare the

146

poet's description of a primrose with the botanist's. They are talking about the self-same object. But one shows the feelings of a sensitive person as he looks at it, and the other tells about its intricate construction, its relationship to other plants, and that sort of thing. Are the poet and the botanist contradicting each other? Scarcely. They are both talking sense. They are both talking truth. But they are talking on different levels of truth. One addresses your intellect, the other your heart.

The invasion of Gog represents a truth, a profound and important truth, but it is not the same kind of truth that is represented by the invasion of Nebuchadnezzar in Chapter 21, where Ezekiel shows by grim pictures that Nebuchadnezzar will fall upon Jerusalem with his horrible engines of war, and the walls of the city will crumble. Here he is telling us something very different. He is using the invasion of an imaginary character to picture the spiritual safety of the person who lives his faith.

Some students of the Bible seek, and inevitably find, predictions about modern history in Ezekiel. One such author wrote, "It is universally agreed that chapter 38 is the Russian chapter." The statement might more accurately have read, "It is universally agreed among a vocal minority that chapter 38 concerns Russia." To be sure, Ezekiel uses an unusual expression "chief prince." (There are more unusual expressions in Ezekiel than in any other book of the Bible.) His word "chief" is *rosh*. Some versions translate the phrase, "Gog, prince of Rosh." We do not know any nation in Ezekiel's time that was called Rosh. (There is a great deal about Ezekiel's time that we do not know.) For that reason, are we justified in making the gigantic leap from *rosh* to Russia? Every other time the word *rosh* occurs in the Bible it means "chief" or "head" or something of the sort.

The great majority of biblical students, both Hebrew and Christian, believe that Chapters 38 and 39 are not prediction, like Chapter 21 that foretells Nebuchadnezzar's attack on Jerusalem, but they are an entirely different kind of writing, what we call "apocalypse," a Greek word that means taking away the veil. The Latin word for the same thing is "revelation." The best known example of such writing is the last book in the Bible. Ezekiel is sometimes called the father of apocalypse because this section in his prophecy is the earliest known example. Between the time of Ezekiel, exiled in Babylon, and the time of John, a prisoner on Patmos, were thousands of other apocalyptic writings. I have examined a few of those that remain. Some are glorious, most are dismal.

In apocalypse, the appeal is to the imagination. Everything is giant size. The writer makes little attempt to trace logical connections from one event to another. Dream-like phantoms fade and are replaced by other phantoms. The action usually is violent. All the colors are vivid and glaring. Yet the faces, more often than not, are blurred; so we cannot tell whom they represent. The time likewise is vague, and so are the locations. Obviously, within a framework like this, a second-class writer could produce a first-class bore, and many succeeded. But in the hands of a man of faith and deep intellectual power, like Ezekiel or John, this difficult type of writing can be packed with meaning.

What sets apocalypse aside from other kinds of writing is that ideas are pictured as events. Gog represents every evil, not a particular king. Magog is every source from which evil comes, not a particular territory near the Caspian. I have heard the cry, "Are you saying this isn't true?" And my answer is, "Yes, it is true. Like every other kind of truth, it must be examined on its own terms." It is possible, you know, to count the calories in a diamond, or to measure the light refraction from a potato. The result of your measurement might be true, if you did the work skillfully enough, but it would not be the kind of truth in which most of us are interested.

People have tried to identify Gog with all sorts of historical characters. The leading candidate for the dubious honor is Gyges, king of Lydia in Asia Minor, who was known as Gugu in the Babylonian records. It is hard to believe that anyone ever feared a man named Gugu, but the historical records show him a cruel, successful warrior.

Likewise, people solemnly play the numbers game, proving to their total satisfaction that the beast in Revelation, whose number is 666, represents this or that modern tyrant. Once, just to see if I could, I decided to prove that the beast represents Adolph Hitler. I assigned a numerical value to each letter, and juggled the figures around casually, and in ten minutes I had my "proof." I could have done it in a short time, but the telephone rang. To be sure, I had to use the number 7 to represent the "g" in Shickelgruber. But my reasoning was no more fantastic, and no more distant from the biblical intent, than the antics of some enthusiastic abusers of prophecy.

After all these things have been said, the apocalypse in Ezekiel is about Russia, or at least about the evil powers in Russia that have tried to stamp out the Church of Christ, and are trying to subvert and destroy decent government whereever possible. And the number of the beast, 666, does represent Adolph Hitler. Gog and the beast are different names for the same reality. The reality is the hatred for the Lord and His people that has existed down through the ages, and exists today, and will continue to exist until the final victory over every power that is arrayed against God.

WHAT IS THE APOCALYPSE ABOUT?

In every troubled century, on every troubled continent, the picture of Gog's defeat while attacking Jerusalem has brought strength and courage to troubled people. When Ghengis Khan and his golden horde were invading Christendom, Christians read this passage and realized that God would be victorious, not Ghengis. For centuries the Saracen ruled over Christians in Europe. And during that entire time those who followed the Nazarene were enabled to keep on following Him because Ezekiel helped them with his eerie apocalypse. When tragedy of any kind stares you in the face, call it Gog, and look to the Lord of Hosts who will be the Victor.

Today Gog is named Mao Tse Tung. He is a man of brilliant intellectual gifts and incredible ability to achieve, who is led by a deep and doubtless sincere concern that people have enough food and other material necessities. He believes that he knows the way to bring these good things to people, and he is perfectly willing to kill, or torture into submission, anyone who disagrees with him. He has a passionate hatred for Christ and His Church because, he claims, we teach people to long for pie in the sky by-and-by instead of working with him to build a paradise upon earth. Christians, who have not taken the trouble to read their Bibles thoughtfully, ask

me, "Do you think the Church can stand before the attacks
of Communism?" There is little point in my answering the
question. The Lord Himself has answered it, in the thirty-
eighth and thirty-ninth chapters of Ezekiel.

Gog has other names, as many names as evil has faces. Call
him juvenile delinquency. Call him marital infidelity. Call
him alcoholic addiction. Do you notice how much nicer sin
sounds when we talk Latin? It's all sin. Call it Gog. That's
what Ezekiel's talking about. That, and the Lord's victory.

A faceless and nameless form of evil abroad in our society
represents a greater threat to faith than does Mao or any of
the sins that we so eloquently discuss in Latin. I do not know
a single word to describe this attitude, but I could point you
to any one of fifty novels or plays that have been successful in
recent years and say, "Here is the picture of Gog." These
works are written with infinite skill, by writers who look at
modern life and portray what they see. In the process they
help to create what they describe: a life that is essentially
meaningless.

We Christians ask the Lord for our daily bread. If that is all
we want, then life has no meaning. Substitute sirloin steak
or a split level trap (and I didn't invent that expression) you
still have a meaningless life. Exalt man's desires to any material level you can imagine: a scientific discovery, a symphony
composed, a corporation organized. Then invite man to
fulfill his desires. If that is all life means, life still is restless
and incomplete. Contemporary writers show people who are
striving, successfully or unsuccessfully, for a fast buck, and
spending the buck, if they can get it, on sensual pleasures,
because there is nothing else to spend money for. I do not
consider the description edifying, but I believe it to be accurate. I talk with such people almost every day.

Back in the 1920's writers proposed that we throw away
the shackles of Victorian morality and everyone would be
happy. Such was the face of Gog forty years ago. The particular attack was against the ideal of purity in the relationship between men and women. Christians opposed the libertine movement, as we must oppose every movement contrary
to God's will, and were called narrow-minded, blue-nosed
kill-joys. The proponents of libertine action received a more

enthusiastic audience than did those who upheld the divine standard. The same thing was true in the days of Moses, Elijah, Ezekiel, or Jesus; all of whom upheld the standard of purity in human relationship and were laughed at for doing so.

Something interesting has happened. The proposed experiment has been tried, and brilliant authors today are examining the result. I am not thinking now about the cheap motel romances and other pornography. Serious authors are examining the human situation as carefully as they can, and reporting upon it with accuracy, as is their right and duty. No intelligent observer can ignore the fact that the human race comes in two genders, and that complications arise from the difference. I believe that the difference and the complications could be examined without the clinical detail that is so popular today. Shakespeare, Dostoyevski, and Cervantes all deal with human behavior, which includes both the glory and the shame of sex, without delving into the gutter. But now that I've registered my protest, let me add something.

The serious writers who are examining the human situation today show people who have thrown away the shackles, and they report with clinical exactness what it means to live without moral direction. Such is the face of Gog today. Back in the twenties they told us that if we did this we would be happy. Now people are doing it, and I defy you to find in this world's literature a more miserable bunch of neurotic self-haters than the dismal people who live in the dismal suburbs of the contemporary novel or play.

I have said that I talk frequently with the kind of people whom modern authors are describing, people without a goal, who are living for their own desires, who have made their beds in hell. One day, a few years ago, the schedule worked out so that I spent seven hours talking with people who had just been divorced or were about to be divorced. None of them, by the way, was a practicing Christian. The evening, for some odd reason, was free. I had read that the film *The Misfits,* by Arthur Miller, was brilliantly done; so in lamb-like innocence I went and found myself listening, almost verbatim, to the sort of thing I had spent all day hearing. Only this time I was paying for it.

I don't spend all my time talking with failures. My work is with the Christian Church, the people whom Gog is trying to destroy. The members of the Church have the same kind of difficulties anyone else has. They have the same kind of desires and temptations. And occasionally one of them slips and falls. But there is a difference. They know where they are going. If they fall, they get up and start again, in the right direction. And while they are on the way, they know a happiness that the troops of Gog never imagine. Jesus said, "These things I have spoken to you, that my joy may be in you, and that your joy may be full." He delivers what He promises, to those who have forgotten about joy, forgotten about self, and are doing their best to carry out His will. In the process they have found their true self and incidentally have found great happiness. This is Christ's victory over Gog.

WHERE IS MAGOG?

Where does Gog come from? That's easy, Magog. Where is Magog? You might be surprised how much erudite brainpower has been expended trying to give a geographical answer to this spiritual question. Perhaps Ezekiel invented a word to mean the land of Gog, perhaps there was a vaguely defined region called Magog in the never-never land to the north. It doesn't matter, if the Son of Man is writing an apocalypse.

In one place the Lord says to Gog:

> Thoughts will come into your mind, and you will devise an evil scheme and say, "I will go up against the land of unwalled villages."

This couldn't be much clearer. Evil people think up devilish schemes. It's been going on for a long time. Many evil people are around, and they can invent infinite deviltry.

In another verse the Lord says to Gog:

> I will turn you about, and put hooks into your jaws, and I will bring you forth, and all your army.

No, Ezekiel is not contradicting himself. He is talking about the mystery of human freedom in a world where the eternal God is Ruler. You find the same contrast written up in the Book of Exodus. One time it says that Pharaoh hardened his heart. The next time it says the Lord hardened Pharaoh's heart. When God hardened Pharaoh's heart, Pharaoh was making up his own mind, on the basis of his own wisdom and prejudices, just the way we do. He did not realize that, all unwitting, he was the agent of divine Providence. Ezekiel tells us much the same thing: not that evil strikes innocent people — anyone with half an eye can see this — but that divine Providence is working when earthly events seem to us utterly hopeless.

Divine Providence does not mean for one moment that the Lord overcame Gog's freedom of the will, or Pharaoh's, or Ghengis Khan's, or Adolph Hitler's. The most clear-cut example of divine Providence working through people who were hostile to God was at Jesus' trial and crucifixion. Neither Caiaphas nor Pontius Pilate dreamed that their action, taken upon their initiative, was to be the central event in the Lord's plan of salvation. But it was.

Magog is wherever human thought defies the divine will. Let others, if they will, discuss its geography. At least they are not getting into serious mischief while asking a question without a sensible answer. You can profit by asking the one sensible question about Magog: "Lord, is it in me?"

THE VICTORY OVER GOG

The Apostle has summed up Ezekiel's message:

> In everything God works for good with those who love him . . . Who shall separate us from the love of Christ? Shall tribulation, or distress, or persecution, or famine, or nakedness, or peril, or sword? . . . No, in all these things we are more than conquerors through him who loved us.
>
> Romans 8:28-37.

Paul's expression is addressed to your intellect, Ezekiel's to your heart, down deep inside you, where your basic attitudes are formed. Later on these attitudes crop to the surface, where your mind gives them some intellectual trimming and scrubbing.

What is Ezekiel saying in words of fire? First that evil is abroad in the world. As far as I am aware everyone but the Christian Scientists will agree to this. Second, that God is working even when evil threatens to overwhelm and destroy Him. A great many people will shake their heads sadly and turn away from this idea. They haven't heard — way down deep — that God conquers through a Cross. But Ezekiel does not leave us with a nice warm feeling that somehow things are going to turn out all right in the end. He is a recruiter, not a salesman for tranquilizers. In the third place Ezekiel calls us to the moral struggle. He says that your life counts. Your moral victories count. You can take part in God's final victory.

Now do you see why I said that the modern cult of the meaningless life is really more dangerous to Christian faith than is Communism? The Communist is at least taking part in the moral struggle. He hates you, and invites you to hate him. He is trying to overcome you with evil. You are supposed to be trying to overcome him with good. But the modern cult of the meaningless says there is no moral struggle. There is no right or wrong. There are only desires. Fulfill yours if you can. It will not make you happy or good or anything old-fashioned if you succeed, but try anyway.

The moral struggle matters. If you are a general, faced with the question of dropping a nuclear bomb, it matters what you decide. If you are the governor of a state, and your actions will determine whether the forces of hatred or those of law will decide questions of civil rights, the moral struggle matters. Most of us are not quite so high up the social scale. But we are a great deal higher up than were the exiles to whom Ezekiel talked.

Your moral struggle matters. Be it in the back seat of a parked car. Be it keeping that sharp tongue reined in. Be it only a friendly word to the person on the other side of the barrier — any barrier. Be it the question to cheat or not to cheat on the examination. Be it keeping or returning the extra dollar that was folded into your change. It matters what you decide. This is where God's victory is won, in the hearts of people. God cares what you are. God cares what you do.

If all this sounds faintly familiar, it is. The same Holy Spirit who guided Jesus' earthly life likewise guided the earlier Son of Man. Jesus lived the truth we have been talking about, and was butchered for living it. But, as Ezekiel has told us, the Lord defeated Gog — his name was Caiaphas in those days. Jesus rose from the dead. He lived the truth that Ezekiel is talking about. And the night before He died he wrapped it all up in one sentence:

In the world you have tribulation; but be of good cheer, I have overcome the world.

John 16:33.

Ezekiel 47:1-12

[The guide] brought me back to the door of the temple; and behold, water was issuing from below the threshold of the temple toward the east (for the temple faced east); and the water was flowing down from below the south end of the threshold of the temple, south of the altar. Then he brought me out by way of the north gate, and led me round on the outside to the outer gate, that faces toward the east; and the water was coming out on the south side.

Going on eastward with a line in his hand, the man measured a thousand cubits, and then led me through the water; and it was ankle-deep. Again he measured a thousand, and led me through the water; and it was knee-deep. Again he measured a thousand, and led me through the water; and it was up to the loins. Again he measured a thousand, and it was a river that I could not pass through, for the water had risen; it was deep enough to swim in, a river that could not be passed through. And he said to me, "Son of man, have you seen this?"

Then he led me back along the bank of the river. As I went back, I saw upon the bank of the river very many trees on the one side and on the other. And he said to me, "This water flows toward the eastern region and goes down into the Arabah; and when it enters the stagnant waters of the sea, the water will become fresh. And wherever the river goes every living creature which swarms will live, and there will be very many fish; for this water goes there, that the waters of the sea may become fresh; so everything will live where the river goes. Fishermen will stand beside the sea; from Engedi to Eneglaim it will be a place for the spreading of nets; its fish will be of very many kinds, like the fish of the Great Sea. But its swamps and marshes will not become fresh; they are to be left for salt. And on the banks, on both sides of the river, there will grow all kinds of trees for food. Their leaves will not wither nor their fruit fail, but they will bear fresh fruit every month, because the water for them flows from the sanctuary. Their fruit will be for food, and their leaves for healing."

THE RIVER THAT TRANSFORMS
THE WILDERNESS
Ezekiel 47:1-12

During the past week at least a dozen members of the Church have said, as pleasantly as possible, "I'm glad you're finishing with Ezekiel." One of them added, "When you're talking about it, somehow it sounds all right. But you asked us to read the book. And my wife and I read a chapter and I look at her and say, 'Does this make any sense to you?' And she says, 'No.' Then we read another chapter and go through the same procedure."

I remind you, I never promised that Ezekiel would be an enjoyable book. I did promise that, if you will examine the message with care, you will find it packed with hope. Ezekiel is a profitable book. Diamond miners, you know, must go through an unconscionable amount of blue clay per diamond, and Ezekiel contains at least its share of blue clay. I have tried to read nothing into Ezekiel that isn't genuinely there. I have tried to draw from Ezekiel various messages that troubled people in the twentieth century need to receive. If this much has been accomplished, it is enough. I do not ask that you enjoy reading Ezekiel.

The forty-seventh chapter in this obscure, antagonizing, but profitable and hopeful book is about a river that starts at the Temple in Jerusalem and flows down through the Arabah to the Dead Sea, and transforms the bleak desert into a fertile garden.

THE ARABAH

To the east of Jerusalem the land is rugged. A huge geo-

logical fault runs through central Palestine. At the depth of
this fault, eighteen miles east of Jerusalem, is the Dead Sea,
the lowest known spot on the surface of the earth. Its surface is 1292 feet below the Mediterranean level. Since Jerusalem is on a ridge about half a mile above sea level, the
difference in elevation is almost three-quarters of a mile. If
my long division is correct, that gives an average gradient of
four per cent. The gradient is seldom average. It is cut
through with canyons and gullies. Moisture laden clouds
from the Mediterranean blow over Palestine. As the land
rises, the moisture is condensed and falls. To the west of
Jerusalem is rainfall. To the east is almost none. So the
desert Ezekiel is talking about is a rugged, barren land.

You remember reading about the lads who found the Dead
Sea Scrolls? They were smuggling goats from Transjordan
into Palestine. They detoured south of the bridge to avoid
the border-guards. And, as Edmund Wilson says in *The
Scrolls from the Dead Sea:*

> They had come to the Dead Sea in order to stock up with
> water at the spring of Ain Feshka, the only fresh water to
> be found for miles in that dry, hot and desolate region.
> They were quite safe from discovery there: it was a locality
> that had no attractions, to which nobody ever came.

Through the Arabah flows the Jordan. As rivers go, it
isn't very impressive. In eastern Kentucky is a waterway called
Troublesome Creek, that looks just the way it sounds, and
the Jordan closely resembles it. It goes tumbling and splash-
ing through narrow valleys, over rocks that have been rounded
by centuries of its flow. From an airplane the Jordan valley
is one of the most impressive sights you can imagine. You
fly over dull grey-brown jagged hills and gullies — they call
them jebels and wadis — looking at death. Then you come
to the Jordan. A jagged streak of emerald cuts through the
desolate landscape. Here and there a skillful engineer has
channeled some life-giving water to a relatively flat field,
which is verdant and fruitful. It grieves me to tell you that
Jordan oranges command a better price in the European
market than do Florida oranges. We have abundant rainfall,
but few minerals in the soil. The Arabah is rich in minerals
but poor in water. Where the water reaches is life and beauty
and productivity.

The turbulent Jordan today is causing a bitter feud. Israeli engineers have designed an irrigation system to use water from the Sea of Galilee, which would inevitably affect the river's flow. The Jordanians have threatened war if the Israeli begin drawing the water. At present the Israeli are "testing" the irrigation works, and the whole issue is tangled and confused.

All this history and geography will help — I hope — to understand what Ezekiel is driving at. He is talking about spiritual truth in geographical terms. He is not talking about the irrigation project that may prove to be political dynamite. The river that transforms the wilderness is not the Jordan. And the wilderness is not really Arabah at all, it is a symbol for the spiritual desolation in which millions upon millions of people are living today.

Is all this about a desert just preacher-talk about human nature? Admiral Arleigh Burke is no preacher. He is a competent, dedicated, hard-headed Naval officer. And in an issue of *Newsweek,* discussing the state of the nation, he said, "People are just not willing to be involved." He told how a woman was attacked in New York City, while a hundred people watched, and nobody lifted a finger to help her. I can only apologize to the Arabah.

David Riesman is an outstanding sociologist. His study, *Faces in the Crowd,* examines with critical sympathy what modern civilization has done and is doing to people. His technical, almost arid, prose pictures a desolation more lonely than the Arabah.

> With the coming of relative abundance the undiscovered frontiers change their nature: they become more inward, more internalized, more interpersonal, and hence more intrapersonal. Success on such a frontier, however, is impalpable by its very nature—or rather by *our* very nature, which has in the past placed its stress on the world of hard, external "reality.". . . We sense that new possibilities of happiness, by work or windfall, may be open to us, but the resultant anxiety produces an anomie. . . . The ongoing societal shift . . . implies that parents will raise children for one sort of pioneering while the latter will encounter another sort. Realizing all this, we should be surprised at how low the divorce rate is, not shocked at its size. Industrialization and leisure, higher education and a greater freedom in mores, allow us to make demands on family life and claims for per-

sonal satisfaction and growth that in the past were voiced
only by a privileged few. We have, so to speak, democratized
divine discontent. But while we know enough to be dis-
contented with our human relationships, we do not know
enough—and in some senses, of course, we never will—to
improve them substantially, or even to know where to look
for help.

Jesus said it, somewhat more succinctly, "A man's life does
not consist in the abundance of his possessions." Dr. Riesman shows us a civilization, our civilization, not Ezekiel's,
which provides a lavish abundance, and in which people are
lost, and *do not know where to look for help.*

The book *On Her Majesty's Secret Service* is not a place
where you would expect to find any significant Christian
thought. Even so, Ian Fleming, who is seldom considered a
theologian, once took a long, critical look at the life he
recommended, and he said:

> Men and women . . . burn the heart out of themselves by
> living too greedily, and suddenly they examine their lives
> and see that they are worthless. They have had everything,
> eaten all the sweets of life at one great banquet, and there
> is nothing left.

One final illustration from contemporary life. I am actually
old enough to remember the days when people thought
Tobacco Road a shocking play. It pictures a Georgia cracker,
Jeeter Lester, whose material life is about on a level with the
hogs on his farm, and whose moral life is several cuts below.
Erskine Caldwell, whose father was a Presbyterian minister
in the Georgia hill country, wrote the play, which realistically
describes people whom Mr. Caldwell had known. When it
showed in Atlanta, the Reverend Mr. Caldwell took some
people from Tobacco Road to see it. Their comment after-
ward was, "Wouldn't old Jeeter hev purely loved it?" I look
back on my emotions as I saw that play, during the depres-
sion. It rang the alarm bell in the heart. We've got to help
these people. They need schools, hospitals, roads and decent
jobs. We've got to clean up the mess.

Now come down a third of a century. The smash hit these
days is *Who's Afraid of Virginia Wolfe?* This likewise is an
acute study of people who are living with little or no conscious reference to God. Jeeter Lester was poor. They are
rich. Jeeter Lester lived in filth. They live in immaculate

homes. Jeeter Lester was ignorant. They are doctors of philosophy. And their lives show the same hideous spiritual sterility that Jeeter Lester's showed. Their brilliant intellects are filled with the same kind of spiritual muck. The play is a loud, shrill cry for help. But how can we help these people? Schools? They've attended the best. Roads? They drive around in Cadillacs now. Hospitals? They can afford anything in the world. Jobs? They have good jobs.

Perhaps the suspicion might, just possibly might, slip into your mind that Ezekiel is right after all. He has insisted that man has important material needs. Part of our faith is to provide these for our neighbor, when he cannot provide for himself. But a well-fed barbarian is still a barbarian. A highly educated louse is still a louse. Maybe, in the Providence of God, the literary era through which we are wallowing will awaken us to the fact that man's primary need is for a right relationship with God. The soil of the Arabah is rich. But it does need water to produce crops.

THE RIVER

The river Ezekiel describes is rather unusual. It has no tributaries, only a source, yet as it flows through the dry, thirsty country, it grows in depth and volume and in the help it brings to human need. The other unusual hydraulic peculiarity is that the river flows both downhill and uphill; like the chariot-throne in Ezekiel's first vision, it goes always "straight forward." We don't need more evidence to convince us that Ezekiel is symbolizing the river of divine love, flowing through human life, bringing beauty, usefulness, and health.

The river flowing from the Temple is the love of God. The phrase, you remember, has two different meanings. It means that you love Him, and it means that He loves you.

The psalmist sings, "There is a river, the streams whereof shall make glad the city of God." Perhaps he took the idea from Ezekiel's prophecy. Does your love for God make any difference in your life? The psalmist has suggested one difference it ought to make. Your faith ought to give you joy. Ours, like Ezekiel's, is a cynical time. In his day people made clever remarks about God to cover up the spiritual emptiness within themselves, and the same thing is happening today.

Turn on the television. You hear brittle wit from those who are announced as comics, but you encounter remarkably little genuine humor. Humor requires a standing place. You must know how things are supposed to be put together before you can see that it's been done wrong, like the farmer who looked at a giraffe and announced, "There ain't no such animal." You who believe in God know how things are put together, and you know that in the middle of the muddle God is working out His eternal purpose. You have something to be joyful about.

Ours is a day of tension. So one drug company after another announces that its major profit comes from selling tranquillizers. The tranquillizing drug has a valuable place in the doctor's bag of medicine. I am not disputing this for a second, when I say that people need a quiet center around which the storm can swirl. Lacking this quiet center, they purchase chemical substitutes. Ezekiel is talking about your quiet center with God, where the stream brings fruitfulness and healing and stability to the rich volcanic soil that would otherwise be blown about by every gust of wind.

Your love for God ought to bring direction and purpose into your life. If you don't have anything else to worry about, you might try wondering why President Kennedy thought it necessary to create a commission on the national purpose. We all know that we want more, we want it bigger, and want it faster. Once in a while, though, we have a terrible, disquieting thought. Is it better? What is my purpose? What am I really living for? If I get it, will it be worth the struggle? Where people are consciously living their love for God, these questions are answered. These people who live their faith have the same kind of needs that their neighbors have. They know the same outward tensions. They know the same temptations. They work in the same offices or factories, drive the same kind of cars, wear the same kind of clothes. But there is a difference. They know where they are going. Oh, they have troubles and they make mistakes. Sometimes they lose the way. But when this has been said, the person who loves God has a purpose for living. He tries to translate his love into practical terms, in dealing with neighbors who are not always loveable.

Your love for God is called faith. His love for you is called grace. It doesn't much matter whether we call Ezekiel's river the stream of faith or the stream of grace. In Christ the two are bound into one. You love God. That means you know where the river is flowing. God loves you. That means the river will reach its destined end. At Christmas time we sing lustily, "He rules the world, with truth and grace." Sometimes we forget. The desert is so wild and trackless. Sometimes we are lost. God isn't. He knows the way. And He's going to get there. He has told us to overcome evil with good. He is in the process of doing it.

Let's forget for a minute about the desert and the river, and in bald, factual terms discuss what Ezekiel is talking about. Forty centuries ago God made a promise to Abraham, that those who shared his faith finally would inherit the earth. During almost every one of the intervening forty centuries, it has seemed to some that the promise was about to be forgotten. The children of Israel went into slavery in Egypt, but God delivered them. They were exiled in Babylon, where Ezekiel called them to be faithful. They were, and God delivered them. Centuries later, the hopes and fears of all the years were concentrated in the life of one Man, who was crucified. But He was not destroyed. The Church He founded had the worst possible start, but it grew. It has known opposition, hatred, and persecution, but it is still here, still growing. Today people by the hundred million are living their faith in God. They are going about the business of being Christian. The cynics sneer that God is dead. They demonstrate that the cynics have it wrong. The world without God is dead. Look at it. Where human love responds to divine love, there is the only genuine life on earth.

THE TEMPLE

The river flowed from the Temple to transform the desert. The last eight chapters of Ezekiel are about the Temple that stands in the midst of the redeemed land. These chapters are packed with rich, meaningful symbolism, telling that worship is man's central business in life. Ezekiel has showed us, in his opening vision, that the reality of worship can take place anywhere, even by the River Chebar. But common sense and spiritual history show that the reality is most likely to take place in the hearts of people who have the valuable habit of coming to worship in a dedicated place. Ezekiel says this by describing at length a Temple building.

From the infinite care that Ezekiel uses in picturing the Temple, we would expect the river to be at its greatest depth in the Temple area, perhaps right beside the sacred altar. Ezekiel knows better, if we don't. In the Temple area the stream of divine love is just a trickle. It shimmers across the courtyard and through the eastern gate. A quarter of a mile, and the rill is beginning to be recognizable as a stream. Another quarter of a mile and it is up to the prophet's knees. By this time the stream has flowed down a steep hill, up another, over the Mount of Olives, and is descending the eastern slope. Twice more the guide measures the stream, and at a distance of a little more than a mile it is too deep to wade.

Ezekiel sees lush vegetation along the banks, and the guide describes to him the farther reaches, where the healing, life-giving waters reach into the Arabah. At the depth of the Arabah is the salt-filled Dead Sea, salty because it has no outlet, lifeless because it always receives and never gives. The healing river transforms this sea from sterility and death into fruitfulness. Ain Feshka — Ezekiel called it Engedi — becomes a prosperous city.

Where does the love of God really count? Ezekiel has told us that public worship is an important part of life. He scarcely would have devoted one-fifth of his prophecy to describing a building, if he did not think it important that people come to such a building and participate in the service. God created man for worship, in which the building and the service are aids. When we have sung our hymns and said our prayers, we are not done with God. The other Son of Man tells us, with painful vividness, that we can go through the motions of worship and deny with our actions everything we have just done and said. It's your life God wants, not a few moments of reverent silence.

As far as you and I are concerned, this Church building represents what the Temple represented to Ezekiel. The miracle of worship is more likely to begin here than in any other spot. But if worship ends here, there is no miracle.

Worship is complete when you have offered your life to God. What happens in this building is worship if it is fulfilled in your office, on your farm, in your shop, in your schoolroom, in your home.